Clipped Wings

Hear the soaring voices set free

Jennifer Gilmour

Thank you for your
support.

Jennifer
G.

CLIPPED WINGS

First published in 2017 Jennifer Gilmour

This is work of non-fiction however some names have been changed to protect the identities of those mentioned.

The contributors are from all over the world and regional spellings may occur in their accounts.

A CIP catalogue record for this book is available from the British Library ISBN 978-1-9999647-0-2 (Neilsen UK).

Published by Pict Publishing

CONTENTS

Dedicated to all those who have supported me on my journey and who want to fly with me. To my husband, without your ability to see the light in such dark times I wouldn't have gained the strength and courage to fly.

And most importantly to all those people who support other survivors. May they know that that their support is valuable, imperative, and appreciated.

INTRODUCTION

The following pages contain personal stories, recounted me by a selection of people, all of whom have suffered the ignominy of domestic abuse. These accounts have been passed to me in response to the publication of my debut novel *Isolation Junction* and the publicity surrounding it. Since then, I have been contacted by dozens of people wanting to share their experiences with me and as a result, I decided that I would do everything in my power to give these people a public voice.

Sadly, many of these stories have similar themes and support the statistic that 1 in 4 women and 1 in 6 men have been affected by domestic abuse during their lifetime.

Each account represents a personal experience and I believe this is key to bringing awareness of this insidious and damaging behaviour. In some cases, people have written their own account, in others, their story has been developed through a personal interview. These are not my words but the words of the brave survivors who have chosen to share their experiences with you.

We hope that this book will be of interest to a broad range of people: professionals seeking to read case studies; people with a specific interest in or training in the sector; those wishing to gain an understanding of what domestic abuse can look like from the victim's point of view so that they may realise that what they are going through is not acceptable.

Whatever your personal reason for reading these accounts, it will aid your understanding and knowledge; these stories are raw and real. You will be given a snapshot of what life was like for them in their abusive relationships.

My hope, therefore, is that this book will empower others to take a stand against this kind of behaviour and see that there are many aspects that make up domestic abuse, from the horrific visuals of violence, the mental torture of emotional abuse and coercive control, the terror of sexual abuse, the worrying financial control, and the disturbing use of children as weapons.

I have also contributed. This is as a mark of solidarity and to send a clear message – those of us who have suffered at the hands of others stand together and by doing so, our voices are louder and our influence stronger.

'Our wings were clipped, our restrictions were made, our boundaries were tested but now we are free, aren't we?

We look above in the sky at the birds and hope to be free. But the birds make their nests in the trees high above, to protect themselves from predators. Free birds must keep looking over their shoulders the same way all of us have to.'

JENNIFER GILMOUR
LIFE AFTER DOMESTIC ABUSE

I used to wonder if I would ever have a life. In fact, I wondered this every day for the five long, lonely years that I lived in an abusive relationship. In the end I didn't care because I was so numb, but here I am now and I want to share with you a snippet of my story.

If you are wondering why someone didn't intervene, let me tell you that there are/were no scars; there were no bruises, in fact, there was no obvious physical evidence that anything was wrong. The scars and bruising were real though ... in my mind. I wasn't hit or kicked, in fact, sometimes I wish I had been as that would have brought some sort of end to the crazy mindset the man I thought loved me, persuaded me to believe about myself.

When we first got together things were normal. Well, I think they were but as I look back I am no longer sure what normal was in that relationship. To excuse his behaviour, I convinced myself that he was just showing an over-protective love as opposed to obsession and control.

I fell for his easy charm and within a few months became pregnant with my first child, and things changed a lot from there. The episodes of abuse, which had been infrequent at first, became monthly events. To begin with, they would consist of interrogating me in the middle of the night, not letting me sleep, and making me sleep on the floor despite being pregnant. Other behaviours involved locking me in the house and throwing things at me. I had no control over any money and consequently, the debts mounted. I didn't have my family close-by as they live on the other side of the country – I felt alone and trapped. Life progressed in this way until eventually, I wasn't allowed to go out to work. By this time, I had two children and felt isolated and unsure. What could I do? I had no money, few friends, no independence, and low self-esteem, despite having a university diploma.

I felt I had to do something, so I created a business working from home because surely, he couldn't argue with that? Or could he?

As I look back, I realise that if it wasn't for some business friends I made at that time, I wouldn't have found the confidence to change this downward cycle which imprisoned me. As the debts mounted, he agreed that I could get a temporary part-time, job for the Christmas season. I became friends with the manager at my new place of employment. There was something about this man which made me feel able to trust him with what was happening in my life. As I opened up to him, he was concerned to hear of events that were happening and tried to convince me that these were not normal in a relationship.

Thankfully my new friend decided to help me and he became my hero, someone I could talk to before going back home, where I had to act like nothing was wrong. I decided that, with my two children, I was going to leave the husband who was abusing me and move back to my family on the other side of the country. My friend decided he was going to give up his job and move with me and the children. I may have made this sound easy but I can assure you, this was very challenging both emotionally and practically. We did it though, and that friend is now my husband and we have both my children and a baby of our own living all under one roof. I couldn't be happier.

The scars of domestic abuse are often hidden from view but as my confidence and happiness have soared, I have realised that there is help out there and there is a way back to freedom.

CLARA

I met my first partner in 1996. I was fifteen years old when I fell pregnant and was asked to move out by my parents. I moved in to a drug-infested flat with my boyfriend and his four friends. The violence started when he beat my thighs with a baseball bat until they were purple because he said I was looking at another man. He told me if I didn't have an abortion he would throw me to the streets, so I had an unwanted abortion. I was then diagnosed with post-natal depression by the doctor as he said it was because I wanted the baby, so I was put on Prozac (this didn't last long as I felt violent and angry, so it was soon changed to a different anti-depressant). All at fifteen years old.

I was then sold by him and his friend for prostitution; was threatened with a knife by another prostitute, who said it was for my own good. I was nothing but a child! They just moved me to another area. After they did this for a month, selling me four nights a week, my boyfriend decided that maybe I liked it and beat me repeatedly for what they had forced me to do. I spent two years being held under the bathwater, punched, headbutted, stamped on, and suffocated whenever he decided to get drunk or high on drugs. Their flat was in a terrible crime-ridden part of Leeds. I knew robbers, heroin addicts, crack addicts, machete-wielding men – the worst kind of people you could think of – were friends with some of the girls in the next tower block and some became notorious murderers, their crimes all over the newspapers.

I was alone, vulnerable, and terrified and had nobody to turn to, everyone around him was petrified of him. Then, suddenly, the abuse stopped and he didn't hurt me for two years. The drugs stopped and I started to reconcile with my parents; they finally answered one of my calls after I had been ignored for years, as if I was the shame of the family for getting pregnant at such a young age.

Life started to get settled and my boyfriend and I got our own home, away from the flat and crime. I soon fell pregnant with my eldest daughter, so we got married. I felt safe, comfortable, and thought now it was maybe time to get my white picket fence. Then he decided to start the abuse again by headbutting me in the face whilst five months pregnant and on our honeymoon in Turkey, paid for by my family. The abuse continued for another four years. I was not allowed friends, anyway, he treat them so terribly that if they were around, they couldn't stand the abuse from him or couldn't stand watching me being treat so badly. I was self-harming, banging my head against the wall whenever he came to attack me, as this stopped him in his tracks. Once he was shouting at me in the house when his friend was there, when I didn't answer, he kicked me in the head, knocking me unconscious on the floor and causing me to wet myself in the process. His friend attacked him and carried me upstairs, changing my soiled clothes to pajamas and staying until I woke up so that he knew I was safe. The attack left me deaf for a week and with a footprint on my face and ear. I left, but he soon found me, convincing me to go back

The area we lived in became too scary to be there. The riots started in the streets around me, there were violent incidents in the streets and then my boyfriend's old friend found us and started harassing me. When my boyfriend wasn't around he tried to tell neighbours that I was a prostitute. We moved to another part of Leeds and met back up with an old friend and I finally found a friend in Lisa, she was my boyfriend's friends partner. She helped me build up some strength to say, 'no more,' when he turned to cocaine behind my back and was constantly controlling any money that came into the house.

I worked two part-time jobs, while he sat at home doing nothing. I struggled every day, walking our girl to nursery and all I got in return was accusations of affairs at work and the wages I earnt all spent.

That New Year's Eve, we went out with friends and he disappeared all night. I later found out he was snorting cocaine with friends, which explained why he was abusive when he came back, making a scene in front of people in the pub.

On 14 January 2004, I told him to leave and he did! I stayed with a friend for a week, suffering terrible abuse and constant threats over the phone. I know I should have phoned the police, WHY DIDN'T I? When I was brave enough to return home that night, I was in bed, he kicked in the front door, dragging me out of bed where my four-year-old daughter lay with me, taking me downstairs, where he sat me for seven hours, telling me he had come back to kill us both. I was petrified. Thought that that night would be my last. I remember looking at the carving knife in the kitchen, thinking *was this going to be a case of me or him?* I reasoned with him and lied, convincing him we could retry the relationship and when he went out in the morning, I grabbed a backpack, my girl's birthday presents, my daughter, and fled to the nearest community centre, who sent me to a women's aid hostel in another town. I was alone, scared, and felt I had no one to turn to. I was scared if my family knew what he was doing, there would be repercussions and then they would be in trouble, which would then be my fault too.

Bradford 2004 – I lived in the hostel in a strange, scary time, the only contact I had was with my old friend who told me he was hunting for me. He wanted to find me, kill me, and take my daughter. After a couple of months, it calmed down and a contact arrangement was made through his parents for him to see our daughter. One weekend my daughter went to him and he refused to bring her back. The police could not help and I had to start court proceedings. I had made friends with an Irish traveller girl in the hostel and I started a downwards spiral with alcohol and my mental health hit the biggest all-time low. I was told a full residency hearing would have to be held and it could take up to one year, with me only seeing my girl one night a week. I couldn't cope and fell apart, but along came my friends brother to pick up the pieces of broken me.

Within months, he moved himself into my new home, then moved his sister in. Then after a year, wham, he beat me up one night, punching me to the floor and stamping on my head. I was trapped. Very soon after, he moved his other sister in too. His family all seemed to excuse the abuse I was suffering. Their excuse was *he only does it when he's drunk you must wind him up!* I got beaten up if I made his tea or I got beaten up if I didn't. I got beaten up for ringing him to see where he was when he disappeared for hours on end, taking my bank card, spending all the money that came into the house.

11

As part of the court case I was diagnosed with complex post-traumatic stress disorder and depression. I managed to get help for the alcoholism and break my habit. I went through a trial of fact and my ex-husband was proven for prostitution, abuse, and domestic violence and I got my daughter back! But she resented me; she wanted to be with her dad.

Two months later, my partner decided to move his two-year-old nephew in and get residency for him. I was pregnant but suffered a miscarriage, his family accused me of lying for attention. I was soon pregnant again and struggling to cope with two kids, pregnancy, an abusive partner, and no money. He would grab me by the throat, lifting me off the ground, repeatedly kick my body, smash up the house, the internal doors were replaced by his family members repeatedly due to him punching doors at the side of my head to terrify me into submission. He sold everything he could for booze and soon I heard rumours of him cheating, which he obviously denied. I didn't have the strength to battle.

He pinned me against the door in front of my children, including my new baby girl, threw me on the floor to their feet, causing them to scream in fear. His reply was to shut them up, he refused to let me have a sterilisation, told me the gypsy way was to have large families. I fell pregnant again, just after he moved his sick and disabled mother in, and his sister left. I was smashed in the face by a phone when I dared to answer her back if she was putting me down, again … she was constantly putting me down, calling me an English whore who was no good for her son. My family had just disappeared into the background again, my whole focus was surviving and trying to protect my girls. He constantly put my eldest down, telling me I favoured her and I was a terrible mum because sometimes she would scream at him to leave her mum alone. One time, he approached her and I jumped up, throwing him to the floor. I received a bad beating for that. It was the only time I stood up for myself but this time, I was protecting my girl.

I was alone with no one to turn to for help. I just wanted peace and normality for my girls. Yet again, no friends stuck around, he was abusive to them and they could understand why I wasn't allowed out. They didn't want to come to a house where they watched him get drunk and treat me terribly. In 2008, I got pregnant again, but ended up in hospital for emergency surgery due to an ectopic pregnancy. He turned up at my bedside whilst I was on morphine in recovery, he was drunk with my girls in tow. I was too ill to object. I came home and a few months later, I fell pregnant with my third daughter, who was born in 2009. She was about six-months-old when more accusations of him cheating arose. Apparently, this time when I was in hospital due to being ill in my pregnancy, yet again denied by him. A few months later, a friend of his visited and he accused me of cheating. I woke up on the living room floor with the house smashed around me, I was used to running on autopilot so I got the girls dressed for school and nursery and put the baby in the pram, I got half-way to school when my daughter told me there was blood running down my neck, another mum offered to take them to school and I headed home. I had two black eyes by the following day and had found out the bleeding was from where he grabbed my ears to headbutt me in the face, he informed me of this.

His family acted like the injuries were invisible, nobody mentioned the state of my face and I daren't take the girls to school until they were gone. By this time, the police had come to the house for domestic disturbances but I always told them we were fine. I was scared of the repercussions from him and his family. One night, in 2010, he got drunk and went drinking in town, before he left, he verbally abused me, telling me he would find someone better. I was plagued by phone calls all night, his mum had now moved out and even when he wasn't home, she would constantly ring, quizzing me as to his where abouts and asking what I was doing? He returned home at 5.00 a.m., screaming abuse, asking me how dare I go to bed? and rambling about some bitch annoying him. He climbed in to bed and then I heard the door banging, I went down, the police where there saying he was under arrest for rape.

I was dumbfounded, left stood there in a daze. I took the girls to school and went shopping, walking round in a complete daze, unaware of what was happening. Then he returned home on bail, no charges. He said he had not raped anyone but he had cheated on me. I was totally, mentally exhausted and just nodded my head. I buried my head in the sand but as time passed, weeks turned into months and after six months, he was charged with rape.

He disclosed nothing to me, telling me he had met a girl, cheated and that she had lied, that's it. When he was charged, I fell apart. Was my partner a rapist? What were they saying had happened? The police aren't often wrong are they? Did he do this or did he just cheat? Was the girl better than me? Was I the piece of shit they all said I was?

The beatings were getting worse, one night, he refused to let me sleep in bed or on the sofa. He kept calling me to bed and then physically kicking me hard on to the floor. When I went downstairs, he followed, demanding I went upstairs. He did this to me, highly amused, for about an hour, then he made me sleep on the floor, like a dog in the corner. He said it's what I deserved, that I could leave but I would never get out alive with the girls, I had to leave alone. I couldn't do that. We moved to a new house and I finally got my dream home and then the solicitors appointments started.

I then found out that he was accused of oral rape against a deaf twenty-one-year-old girl. He obviously said she was lying, said he had taken her to his family's home, they had made her tea that night after the pub. His family were never loyal to me, it was disgusting. Was I worth that little? I started to wonder, *had the monster I lived with done this?* The beatings and drinking were getting worse. One night, he started beating me and spitting in my face, telling me the other girl was so much better than me, no wonder he cheated. I went to my doctor; my mental health was so bad I asked them to section me and put my girls in foster care. They refused to do that as I was strong enough to request help. Again, I was alone.

He got drunk, causing fights with the neighbours and one night, one of them beat him to a pulp in the street, accusing him of trying to touch his sister. He packed our home into a van and moved us again. I lost my dream home. As the rape case unfolded, I started to believe that maybe he had done it. His name was in the paper. I was hiding in shame, more confined to the house than ever, but I wanted it that way too.

One night he threatened to come home and kill me and take the girls. I packed a bag and ran to the police, they sent me to my mum's in Leeds, but her boyfriend wouldn't let us stay, he put us in a hostel two minutes away from my home back in Bradford. Nobody wanted me, I felt worthless. This was just a homeless hostel where they told me, within a couple of days, that I needed to get my home back. When I tried, I ended up back with him because he said he would leave. That day never came.

My life turned around when the local children's centre turned up at my door saying my youngest daughter was eligible for free nursery and could I come to the centre to discuss it? He allowed me to go. When I got there, I poured out my life story. I finally might have some help, we agreed that there was a large possibility he could go to jail, so we would wait till then so they could help me relocate and start again, but the abuse got worse. I was going to the children's centre every week, to a pretend mum's group, he allowed that, so I filled them in on the constant abuse. One night, he got drunk and attacked me so badly he cracked my skull on the drive way, he blacked both my forearms as I protected my face from his constant blows, he only stopped when my mind finally flipped, I picked up the vertical fan and held it over my head, threatening to kill him if he came back at me. He ran downstairs, my kids were crying in their room, and I gave my daughter my phone and told her if he didn't leave when I told him she was to phone 999. I went downstairs, he swung a baseball bat at my head then walked into the front garden. I quickly locked the door so he couldn't get back in, he kicked it off. The police arrived and I just asked them to take him away, crying in the corner, disclosing nothing. This was my routine now.

The following night he was back and this time, when he came home he forced me to perform a sex act while he punched me into submission. I got up that morning, 7 October 2011, took my girls to school, and went to the children's centre. I told them he had to go and they decided it wasn't safe for me to go back. Whilst I was out, he had worked out I was gone and collected my daughter from school. I was so overwhelmed by this I collapsed and was sent to Leeds, to my mums, in a taxi. She knew nothing about my life and the abuse I had suffered, I was in no fit state to tell her what had happened. I could seek help to get my daughter two days later when the courts opened as yet again, it was a family law matter — *he had rights!*

The next day he contacted my family saying my girl wanted her mum and to come and get her. The police took me and I picked her up. I was given a temporary home after two days in a hotel and I was finally free. He couldn't get to me. He applied for custody of the girls but when it got to court, he said he didn't want the girls, he wanted me back. I stood strong and blanked his looks and words. After two court hearings asking for his evidence statement for the domestic violence accusation, he was given permission to write to the girls. My middle daughter sent him letter saying she was fine, he never replied. The girls were scared, all sleeping in my bed and having night terrors, saying he was coming to get me and kill me. My middle girl started seeing a therapist for support. We were living in a house, a temporary shelter home, we had no furniture or belongings of our own. I spent most of Christmas Day crying and feeling like the worst mother in the world; the girls sitting in the house with only a few gifts. When court came around again, in the New Year, he backed down. He didn't turn up and the case was closed. A no contact and a prohibited steps order was issued preventing him taking the children.

Later that year, he went to trial for rape and a 9/12 jury case was found, causing dismissal as 10/12 is needed for a guilty decision. So, he got away with it. I know he did it because he re-enacted the same night on me. A year later, when my eldest daughter was twelve-years-old, she told me that since the night I went into hospital whilst pregnant, he had touched her inappropriately. The police investigated but because it was her word against his and there was no evidence, the Crown Prosecution Service couldn't charge. He got away with that too.

I spent two years alone, building a home for my girls. I learnt to drive, went to college, and visited a psychiatrist for some therapy, which I am still getting now. I still talk to my children's worker from Bradford to this day (she's my hero). I went through years of trying to find myself, sleeping with men because I wanted to, refusing to have feelings, standing behind the brick wall I built with barbed wire on top. In 2013, I met a lovely man. He started to remove some bricks slowly. We have been together for nearly four years now and have been married for two. He's gentle and kind, the girls call him Dad, they love him dearly. My eldest couldn't cope with all the stuff that happened, so she went to live with her father and step-mother. We have a great relationship now.

I have reconciled with my family but never have been able to tell them my story, I don't want to give them some of my pain too. I will never tell them about this book.

I've got a job now, after spending lots of time in therapy and rediscovery. I never knew what life as a free person was. I was abused from the age of fifteen, now I'm thirty-six. I still take lots of medication but am stable. Complex post-traumatic stress disorder is the label and chain around my neck I'm left with, I'll always have nightmares, flashbacks, feelings of guilt, low self-esteem, hating myself for my past decisions, avoidance etc.

I changed. Something triggered in me. I no longer know what backing down is, I come out physically fighting. I don't have that flight or fight response anymore. I'm scared of what could happen if I'm scared and threatened again but I'm free from abuse, not scared everyday anymore. I've not seen my ex for five years, no contact at all, his family tried to speak to me, and I blanked them on Facebook but that doesn't mean he's gone. Unfortunately, I'm scared and haunted every night in my dreams by what he has done, but I'm not controlled, contained, and abused any more (except inside my mind), I can be me. I'm strong. I'm a survivor. I wish there was a tablet to erase mine and my children's memories. Luckily, my youngest doesn't remember the monster, my middle girl is no longer blinded by the fake memories she created for him, and my eldest is finally reducing therapy and starting a medication reduction.

I'm not the person I was before. I'm a completely different person now, shame it wasn't good things that made me this way!

I want to make a special thank you to my saviour Jaime O'Leary. Thank god you knocked on my door that day, thank you for finally giving me a light at the end of that tunnel. I believe that if you hadn't helped me leave then maybe it could be someone else writing my story as I sit in a cell or lay in my grave. I honestly believe the next beating would have resulted in either my death or his. I can never thank you for everything you have done for us, we love you.

CLAIRE

Int: Could you tell me how you met him and how the relationship began?

C: I was fifteen when I met him, just by chance really, friend of a friend, obviously we got talking and I wasn't really interested but he pursued it. He was a few years older than me so I told him nothing could happen and my mum and Dad said, 'oo you're a bit young.' He said that was fine. So, we left it for a little while and we started going out with each other when I was sixteen, it was a bit, 'Oh I'm sixteen now so it can all happen!' And everything went really fast. He lived out of town so would drive for an hour on a weekend to come and see me, I couldn't drive so he was coming across to stay, generally with my mum and Dad, we would stay in the same house but in separate rooms. And they were quite strict in that we weren't meant to be left alone together.

I was just short of seventeen and we got engaged and, being seventeen, I was so excited, it seemed to be what other members of my family were doing so, I thought it was great. The following October was my birthday and we thought that would make a good date to get married on my eighteenth. But, because on the day, for the license, I wasn't eighteen until later on in the day, we needed parental consent, on my wedding certificate it said seventeen so it was a pointless idea. Obviously, my mum and Dad gave consent, they were more than happy, so that was how we met and got together.

Int: Young love then ... So, what happened then in the relationship? Did it take a turn? When did things start to feel unsettled?

C: I'd say that just before we got married there were a few little things, like he would say, 'You shouldn't be wearing that.' Or, 'We *are* doing this.' I was young but I had a mind of my own and would question or challenge him, but I was quite quickly told, 'We are doing it this way.' So, I would think *well okay* and it would carry on like that. I

18

remember the morning of our wedding and weirdly, I wasn't nervous, I was quite excited about the day itself and everything like that, and I remember my dad – we were literally outside – asking me, 'Are you sure? This is it now, you marry someone for life so, are you absolutely sure?' I said I didn't know and he told me I wasn't doing it then, but I quickly assured him I wanted him, I wanted to do it, it was ok, I didn't have any doubts but ... I was seventeen, I didn't really know my own mind, that was the problem. Looking back, I think yeah, I'd seen some signs but I'd not followed it.

The first thing I saw was on our wedding night really.

The first 'side' of him that I saw, that was picked up by others the next day, so from there it just escalated.

Int: Do you feel comfortable talking about that or ...

C: Yeah ... it was something or nothing ... everything was going all right up until him saying he wanted to give me a love bite. So, I said, 'okay if that's what you want to do,' but it literally took over the whole side of my neck and all the way down, to the point that the next day, when we went to see my parents, I had to wear a polo neck jumper. My mum asked me what was wrong, I told her nothing. I was so badly marked over the side of my neck that I had to hide it from my parents. They kinda figured out what it was and when I told them, they thought it was strange. And that was the first thing, that was the only thing I remember of that night strangely enough, it was the effect of that and obviously the next day, knowing that it was something that I had to hide.

Int: So, after that, did the signs become more often ...?

C: Yeah ... it got to the stage ... I fell pregnant very quickly and that didn't all go to plan, which then caused a big rift between us – understandably. But then as everything started going on, he didn't know how to deal with it and I didn't know how to deal with and I think that caused a lot of friction. I would cry and hide and he would just lash out. It would go from me cooking his favourite meal and, if it didn't have enough salt on, it would be thrown against the wall or the knife would be held against me – I just didn't know which way it was going to go because it could something really silly, like a cooked tea, or it could be something I'd said wrong and it would get physical.

Int: And how did you feel when you were in those situations when he flipped out?

C: Well, when it was something like the tea, because that stands out specifically in my mind, I can literally see the room and exactly how everything was and I stood there saying, 'I don't get it. I don't understand what's going on.' I'd made a nice dinner and I don't understand why you've just thrown it at me because it wasn't something I'd ever seen before. I'd ask, 'Why have you done that?' and he'd tell me it wasn't right but I didn't understand why it wasn't right. And then obviously I wanted to make it right to fix the problem because I wasn't comfortable in that situation ... that wasn't something I'd ever seen before, it wasn't something I'd spoke about. It was something that I wanted to understand so that I could fix it. If it was anything more than that, it got to the stage where I was panicking, I was shaking, I was hysterical, screaming for help, ringing for help and it just went on and on to a stage where I can't ... I wasn't happy ... I can't walk on egg-shells for the rest of my life and it was going to get to the point where he would have ended up killing me. Something was going to happen because he was so strong, something was going to happen and then what? It got to the stage where I needed to do something.

Int: You mentioned you were asking for help, was that screaming for help at the time or did you seek the services of the police or other people like that?

C: I would literally scream for help, especially when anything violent was happening but I also rang the police once, I'd also rung my parents quite a few times and they had it on their answering machine, me screaming down the phone asking for help. My dad came to the house one night, he used to work nights and my mum had rung him worried, so my dad came to the house and as I opened the door, my dad was stood on the doorstep and he was stood behind the door with a piece of glass in his hand telling me not to say anything ... me and my dad were, I don't know how but we had this weird code going on where my dad was asking if I was okay while winking and I was winking back telling him I was fine as he was shaking his head – we understood each other but obviously my husband didn't know what was going on because he was stood behind the door with the piece of glass. So, my dad said, 'Right, okay, love, I'm going to go back to work, I'm not that far away so if you need me just give me a text.' In other words, he was saying, 'I'm going to be literally parked outside if you need my help', but obviously he didn't know how bad it was and I'm there saying I'm okay but shaking my head that I'm not, trying to get that across to him. There were a few situations like that.

Int: So, you obviously spoke to your mum and dad about the situation, did they ever try to intervene or offer support and help in that way?

C: There was a few times where they'd spoke to him or spoke to us both asking how things were going, but not directly, I would say that in their actual company, it was once or twice where he slipped up or said something or bit my head off or threw a glass at me then said, 'Oh, I've knocked that glass over.' And tried to cover his tracks that kind of way and they'd know that didn't make sense and something wasn't quite right there and a few times they'd ask if he was like that a lot and it was at that stage where I thought *do I say something or do I not say something?*

So, I told them that sometimes yes, but I always played it down because I knew that, at the end of the day, their view was that if you married someone, you married them for life and I wanted to make it work. But I was always getting the comment that I was young – maybe that was the problem? But I wanted to make it right to prove to everybody that actually, I can do it. But unbeknown to me about the kind of person he was!

Int: What was the point where the relationship came to an end? Did it come to a point where you thought that this is the last straw?

C: This had been going on for two and bit years from the wedding and it was getting progressively worse. If we went on a night out and he was drinking, that would be a massive problem, I knew that something was going to happen then. And it was progressively getting worse. To the stage that if I didn't do something soon, how far was he going to go?

One night, we were upstairs in the bedroom, I can't even remember what the argument was about but he had literally pinned me to the bed and was trying to get my phone off me and I was like here, just have my phone, what's the problem? But he dragged me off the bed, we had a big freestanding mirror and he literally threw me into the mirror so I was on all fours, covered in glass and he came across and

21

rubbed my head in to it so I was laid with my whole body in the glass and I couldn't get up. At that point, I thought, *is it going to be next time?* because every time was something a little bit worse. So, this time, I'm laid in a full pane of smashed glass and I said something like, 'you've hurt me …' or something along those lines and he literally picked up the bedside cabinet and threw it at me and I realised I couldn't cope anymore, I needed to go.

That was the night I decided enough was enough.

Following that it took a year till I could actually get out. I saved, secretly, for a year and hid money, which was a massive thing because he lied about money a lot and I didn't understand the concept of how to run a house and things like that so I was basically trying to do anything I could … I did a little bit extra at work, on an evening. Where I was working, a little cleaning job came up that I could do after tea-time so I immediately took it, just anything to try and get a little bit more money and it was almost a year to the day since I'd made the decision, that I said to him, 'Enough is enough and I want you to leave, I want you to go, I don't want you here anymore.' I stood my ground. And somehow, I don't know how or why but he packed a bag and went back to his parents' and said that he'd be back tomorrow when I'd thought about it. I told him there was no point, so I changed the locks. He asked for a single bed and took it. And that was as random as the end actually was. I thought I'd have a huge fight on my hands and I think that, because that year, in my head it was already over, I must have been setting some sort of ground and maybe he sensed that but we never really spoke about it, that was it.

Int: So, when the relationship had ended, did you look for any kind of support or help? You've mentioned there was a huge violent aspect, did you press charges or anything like that?

C: No, I didn't do anything like that and I didn't really talk about it to a lot of people because of the shame of thinking they'd think I'd let it happen, that I should have said something earlier and all the other questions that go around in your head. I did keep it very quiet and I only mentioned it to a few very close friends who knew what was going on, and I told them it was done, he was gone and that was it, I wasn't going to let it happen anymore, I don't know what's going to happen next, I can't risk it, it's my own life. I found support in those few people, especially over the next few months. He showed up one day and told me he'd been on a training course and cheated on me, so I told him good, it was fine by me as he'd already left and I was happy that he wasn't trying to chase me, it was fine. He was only telling me because he wanted back but I told him no, that's it, I'm not interested.

So as random as that was, he thought I'd get jealous I suppose and decide I'd made the wrong decision. From us breaking up, it was six months when he'd filed for divorce stating it was all my fault, that was it really, it went through quite quick. We are randomly in touch about the house and things, but that's it.

Int: What's the situation like now?

C: Strange. I haven't seen him, when he left that day, he came back a few days later to collect a few bits and I haven't seen him since that day. I haven't bumped in to him or anything, which I find really strange as we shared so many friends. He's still in touch with my parents, which is strange but I've never seen him, which is fine by me. Usually, once a year on a specific date, he will message to say that he's thinking about me and I'll reply saying, *'thank you, I hope you're well,'* to keep it quite amicable. Mainly for the fact that it has been a long time and it's my way of closure. Because I've never … he left that day and he came back when someone else was in the house so we've never had that, 'This is way, this is what happened, this is how it made me feel. You shouldn't do that again, I hope you've learnt from the situation.' I can think about it like that now, whereas a number of years ago, I couldn't be like that. I don't know what I'd do if I ever saw him, that would be a completely different story, it's quite easy over text message! If I actually saw him, I don't know how I'd react at all.

Int: What about your personal life?

C: Things have changed, I've learnt so much and I'm a completely different person now. I'm remarried, I've got children, I'm happy. Even if we … it's very rare that we argue which I find a bit strange but if we were to disagree on something I'd just say, 'Right, I've made my point, you've made your point, let's just leave it at that.' Whereas before I would have been very much, 'Oh, that's okay I understand …' but now, I have grown some balls as it were and I do know how to stand up for myself and I will say what's on my mind, rather than sitting in a corner shaking and thinking *if I say the wrong thing, what's going to happen?* I know that's not going to happen now so I can voice my opinion and say, 'actually, I don't believe that, I don't think you're right, I think you're wrong.' And we will laugh about it! So, things are completely different. I never, ever thought, when the marriage was all over, and the way I'd been treat in that situation, I just thought all men were like that and it took me a long time to trust somebody and to trust somebody enough to live with them and have children with them and do normal things because I always thought *well, if I cook a meal and it's wrong, will it get thrown back at me?* Whereas now, it's a joke in our house that I'm not the cook. And if I try to cook, we joke about what this experiment or concoction is going to be! It's always a bit of banter, whereas if I compare it to years ago, if *he* didn't like it ... but now I'll just say that I'm not the chef, he is and we laugh and joke it off.

Things are completely different now, I'm a completely different person, people from years ago who knew us as a married couple who now know me separate from that situation, married with my children, will comment that I am so different, physically, mentally ... I've got a sense of humour now, I didn't have a sense of humour before! I was this boring girl that sat in the corner but now I'm not bothered, I live for today and if I'm not happy, we sort it out and if there's something that's playing on my mind, we sort it out and if we can't, we move away and forget it. I'm quite simple minded about it now because it's easier when you're out.

Int: Well thank you for sharing this, to see that you look at it quite strategically is brilliant and for you to make light of it, just shows that time is a great healer. You've done a complete 360 ... How are things in your new marriage? Do things from that relationship still affect things in your new marriage?

C: In some situations, it will flash back up, but generally it's more ... not with my current husband and the way he is because he's great and he understands and he's very careful but more if we go out on a night and I see violence starting to brew or something, I then will start panicking and think it will come towards me and start worrying what I'll do and I'll get stressed out, so in those situations, it does affect us and we will remove ourselves from those situations. I've suffered with depression and had counselling because of it and been on medication, I do still struggle with anxiety and depression and not necessarily because of how things are now, because if you look at things from the outside it's fine, we have our little ups and down's and spats but generally it's fine, it's everything … but without my past I wouldn't be who I am today, without my past I wouldn't be with my husband, without my past I wouldn't have my children. I'm not thankful for that happening, by any stretch of the imagination, but I've managed to get my head around that if that hadn't happened, as awful and as horrific as it was and I hated every minute of it and would rather have died than being in there, without that, who would I be today? Because it's moulded me to be the person that my husband loves today and now I love myself, and I don't recognise myself, when I look back I think just stand up for yourself woman! What are you doing? What are you sat there for? Tell him where to go. But that's just because of my past, it's cheesy and it's a cliché but that's just how it is.

Life can change.

HELEN FORSTER

I was seventeen when I met my first boyfriend. He was lovely at first but while I was on holiday with my mum, he cheated on me and it broke my heart.

We eventually made up and everything was okay for a while, we moved in to a flat together. He started being violent when he was drunk then he left me for a fifteen-year-old. Not long after, I found out I was pregnant so we decided to try and make it work and got back together.

He was still very violent, smashing the flat up and kicking the door down every weekend, knocking me about and still cheating on me even though I was pregnant.

I reported him to the police on many occasions but as soon as he left the station, he would convince me to drop the charges. The police eventually got fed up of me changing my mind about him – as did some of my friends and family; they grew tired of me going back to him every time I'd swore never to again.

Once I'd had the baby, it didn't take long for things to go from bad to worse. One day, he punched me and broke my cheek bone. This was it, the two-year relationship was over and I eventually managed to cut all ties with him.

I had been on my own for two years when I met my second boyfriend. He was lovely at the start, an older man who took my son on as his own and wanted to settle down and have a family – just what I wanted too.

It wasn't long before he became very controlling and showed his violent side when he was drunk. I lost all my friends, he wouldn't let me do anything. I wasn't even allowed to answer the telephone after 6.00 p.m. on an evening as that was 'our time'.

In time, I fell pregnant but that didn't stop the abuse. He once beat me whilst my son was in the house, I had to run out to a neighbour's house as he had a knife and was trying to seriously hurt me. At a New Years' Eve party, he tried to suffocate me. This time the police took him to court but I couldn't give evidence, so it was thrown out.

I stayed with him and we moved to a new house; a week later, he came home drunk and beat me. That night, my two sons and I left with only the clothes on our backs and I never went back. He continued his abuse towards me by vandalising my car, threatening to kill himself if I didn't go back to him, and raping me, twice. I still stayed away from him and eventually moved into a hostel. We were together for four years before I was finally free of him.

I'd been single for two years when an old friend came back into my life. My boys and I had recently moved and my friend helped me decorate and, not long after, our friendship developed into a relationship. It soon turned sour as he started chipping away at my confidence, telling me that I was fat and ugly and that he had lowered his standards to be with me.

I left him many times but he always came back and pestered and pestered me until I took him back. I got a non-molestation order through a solicitor but I was too weak to keep him away.

One day, he held himself hostage in my house for seven hours, the police had to cordon off my street as he said he had a gun. I still let him back. Eventually, it all got too much and I tried to take my own life. A friend happened to be passing and called in, she found me unconscious and got me to hospital where I was kept in for three days. The whole time he was at my side, brainwashing me to think that I had done it for other reasons. When I left hospital, I was extremely low and he wouldn't leave me alone.

I don't know where I got the strength from but I got in touch with an organisation called Behind Closed Doors and soon started to get help. After four years, I had the strength to leave him for good.

I have been out of abusive relationships for four years now. During this time, I have worked on myself. I threw myself into Thai boxing and fitness and eventually, I started loving myself again.

I have been in a loving relationship for two years now. At first it was hard because I wasn't used to being treat in such a way, but now I am happier than I've ever been before.

Throughout each one of these relationships I have felt scared, exhausted, isolated, ashamed, vulnerable, anxious, depressed, and weak ... even suicidal at times, thinking that I would never have the strength to leave, but I am living proof that *we can survive* – there is help out there and *we will be okay.*

JOANNE HORROCKS

When should you ever feel scared? When your kids dive out in the road? When someone you love gets ill?

I was sixteen and on my work's Christmas night out. I was at a restaurant and this man came walking past and I was in awe, he wasn't extremely handsome but he just hit a cord inside. I used to describe it as *I'd been cold for my whole life and suddenly I felt warmth*. Obviously, things progressed and within six months I was practically living with him. I couldn't be without him, I didn't want to be. I'm thirty-seven now and how I wish I'd read the signs, they were there early on.

We had our first argument within a month. I'd got really drunk at my brother's eighteenth and a lad kissed me, well I was hammered and realised half-way through the kiss it wasn't my new boyfriend. I pushed him away and threw up. Nice – very classy! Well, what do I do? Tell him? I loved him, I didn't want him to go. He knew something was wrong so I confessed and I got called a slag. I must be because he said it, and he loved me as much as I did him, so it must be true.

Well, I know now that was it, that was my first mistake and this let him realise he could say anything to me and I would barely disagree. I have been called a slag for twenty years, the words worsened, my confidence about my appearance was knocked by being called ugly and fat, (I'm a size twelve now and back then eight-ten). Like most lovers, we'd share things in the bedroom. I'd expressed how I would like to kiss, even sleep with a woman – fantasy obviously, this is the bedroom, it's between lovers, it's safe right? No, then the words progressed to lesbian and obviously, because I'm being called these delightful names, the last thing on my mind is sex, so now I'm a frigid as well!

I'm seventeen. I have a miscarriage. No one's fault, actually, quite a silver lining as they realise my insides are weird. I'm eighteen, I'm pregnant again and I'm told that although he wanted the previous one, he didn't want this and if I did, I was going to have to do all the work! I assumed he was just scared, turned out he wasn't lying. I would like to say it was just emotionally that he hurt me, but by this point, things had been thrown, not just by him, me as well, in fact, he was very clever. It was usually me that started it and he'd shout, 'look at you you're always violent, you can't control yourself.' When, in a full-blown argument, if he wasn't winning, he'd bring up anything he could to deflect from the actual problem. 'Your mum's a prostitute, she sold herself for a Dyson, your brother looks like he's got Down Syndrome,' anything to make me pop. I would feel ashamed that I had, so I'd blame myself that the argument had got out of hand. I started it, so it must be my fault.

So, I'm nineteen now, I've had a baby. She is gorgeous but my word, what a shock. I could barely look after myself and now I had this baby. He helped for a few weeks, maybe even a few months but then he started going out. He never went out before, we'd been out once for my eighteenth but now he was going out every weekend. I was exhausted, my daughter didn't do sleep and I really needed sleep. He used to say, 'What have you actually done today? I want a list, I think I should make a list of things that need doing.' I felt like I was useless at everything. I got told I had post-natal depression, the house we'd been renting got repossessed, we were living in a safe house and I felt like I was asking for help – it was just the wrong person I was asking. I'd been given anti-depressants, they were so strong they made me see things. One night, I told him I was going to kill myself, he laughed – his brother was living with us and he laughed too. I went to the bathroom took all the pills … why do they give you so many? I ended up in A & E. My psych evaluation, 'Are you okay? Do you want to do it again?' No – I was released.

Well, that period went from bad to worse, the violence increased, things got broken. I remember one really bad night when his friends were there, I wanted to hurt him as much as he hurt me. I shouted something he'd told me in confidence and for it, I got wrapped in a duvet and kicked. I always had bruises on my arms at this point, apparently from where he'd held me back. Part of it was that I wanted to scratch his eyes out at times but often it was because he'd hold me against the wall, so he could scream how I was fat, ugly, a lesbian, a slag, lazy, a bad mother – he'd spit sometimes … and the words changed slightly. That period ended with the police being called and, for nine months, I was free. I didn't feel free. I loved him and I knew he could be lovely, witty, and charming so I just wanted him back and if I could just change to be better then surely, we'd be okay?

We got back together after I'd slept with someone I used to know – if I'm honest, not really the best choice but he was lovely to me. More ammunition, look at you it's the best you can do.

I'm twenty-one. I get pregnant almost straight away well, knowing I'd be doing it by myself again, I opt for an abortion. My biggest regret in life is that I chose him over my baby. But I was going to do something with my life. I went to college and then university. He hated that I did but he wasn't going to stop me and he was better than when we'd split up, he looked after our little girl loads. He couldn't maintain it for very long and he tried his hardest to make me fail my course, I nearly did, but I kept getting up. There was no way I was killing my baby for nothing, I was going to give the other one a better life.

I got a 2-2 in my degree. Life seemed a bit more stable, I got a proper job and real friends, I'd not had these as an adult before, he always made sure of that. I became a childminder and crazily, I felt that something was missing. I had another baby. But it was going to be great, I work from home so I can do everything.

When I say everything, what do you do for your partner? Well, I had all the bills in my name, except the tenancy, because he hated paperwork, it stressed him out. He hated shopping so I'd buy pretty much his entire wardrobe. Food shop, look after the kids, take them places, occasions, walk the dog, paint the house, mow the lawn, fix small bits … so when I say everything, I mean everything.

Anyway, I'm thirty, I'm complete with my little boy, or am I? Well my ex started sleeping downstairs more and more, he builds a huge shed and starts sleeping in that. I start my own small business, he cannot cope with looking after the kids. I wanted him, I should look after him! I do the majority of the time, but I should have known, he had to come with me a lot. I get an amazing bit of fortune and work for the racecourse, doing what I love – crafts, but there's no way I can take little man.

I find him passed out, it's 4.00 p.m. and there's a bottle of whiskey

31

by him. It's obviously my fault, I expect too much.

Well, I really push it with the money I made and I opened a shop. That's it, he can't cope, total meltdown – I forgot to mention he has his own business that he started up just before I got pregnant with my little boy, he managed this from the fact I'd paid everything for a good six months through childminding from 6.00 a.m. – 7.00 p.m. at times, let's not forget that I'm pregnant! Anyway, he has a breakdown, he lived in the shed for months, his business nearly dissolved.

My first day of opening, he phoned to say he was selling everything and moving abroad to kill himself. He really wasn't in a good place, I wanted to run away but how could you leave someone when they need you most. I stayed. The shop didn't do well, so I gave it back. He amazingly got better.

It sounds odd but his breakdown did me a favour. I coped. I did everything for months – best part of a year. I didn't need him and then one day, the day I call my matrix day, everything changed. We were driving in the car, we'd come around a corner and two guys were walking slowly across the road with cans in their hands, it's about 10.30 a.m.! My ex beeps, one guy says, 'Got a horn, have you?' The next bit I didn't hear, but he supposedly said, with his face at the window, 'I've got a fist.' My ex grabbed his collar and sped off, the guy spun on the spot and fell down. I could see in the mirror – I was mortified. My ex, well, he laughed. Not just a little. At that moment, the floor felt like it opened and everything I'd ever known about this man had gone. How did he not care? That man could have lost his family, be an ex-soldier. He didn't know and he didn't care.

At that moment, I was no longer a slave. I was no longer in love with him. I saw him for everything he was. I tried to stay for my daughter's sake; she'd said she wanted to stay with her dad if we split up. That was in October 2015, on New Years' Eve, I was looking at places to live in Anglesey. I left him on Monday, 13 March 2016. He'd accused me of sleeping with my friend's partner again – a usual tactic to make me lose my friends. I'd feel obliged to say something, as he'd said he was going to and I'd rather they heard it from me. He never actually said anything to anyone, he just didn't want me having friends.

On the Sunday, I'd been to a kid's party. I'd rang Women's Aid,

I wanted out. I didn't get through, I tried again that night but they wouldn't talk because he was in the house. On Monday, I walked down the stairs, he'd slept in the shed, I was trying to sneak out before he got up, he came through the back door with a smirk and said something like, 'why is it I'm in the dog house when it's you that's been shagging around?' I said nothing, I grabbed the dog and I walked out. I saw my friend and burst out crying, I told her the last part and that I couldn't cope, he'd said he wasn't leaving so how do I get out? She was lovely. I phoned Women's Aid again and we talked for a long time. I had said, 'I think I have an option to stay with a friend,' and she explained she couldn't tell me what to do but that in her opinion, it was a good option. I went home and phoned my landlord and told him I was stopping the payments from my bank. I still don't know how I did it, but I literally saw it as taking a walk. Do the most important thing and just keep going.

I will refer back to the question I asked; you should never feel scared to be in your home with your partner.

JODI

My name is Jodi and I've been a Jamberry Consultant since November 2014. When I heard that Jamberry partnered with Fight Against Domestic Violence, I was overcome with so much emotion. I am a survivor of domestic violence.

In 2003, I met a man who I thought was the man of my dreams. He was handsome and charming and he was interested in me. At that point in my life I never thought I would find someone. All my friends were married and having children and I felt so alone. I couldn't believe that I found someone who liked me and was interested in me.

Everything started out great. It was like a fairy tale. He bought me gifts like jewellery and clothing. He was always wanting to be with me. I felt so loved and needed and wanted for the first time in my life. About six months into our relationship, I noticed that he had started to change. I couldn't pin point what it was, but he just seemed different.

I ended up moving in with him. It started off good, but then little things started to happen. I noticed that money started to go missing from my bank account. Some of my more expensive belongings were missing too.

Then I caught him. He was doing drugs. I should have got out then, but I thought I could 'fix' him.

The pain pills soon weren't good enough for him. He started snorting heroine. This is when the violence began. It started with pushing and shoving me ... calling my stupid and worthless. Then it turned into other things. He began forcing me to take drugs like Ecstasy & crystal meth ... Then it was heroine. He'd push my head down and force me to snort it. I would pray that it wouldn't affect me or hurt me.

Looking outside of the situation now I think, *why didn't I just leave?* At the time, I was so scared of him. Still, in my mind, I thought I could fix it all.

Forcing the drugs on me continued, I was in places that I would have never dreamed that I'd be. Crack houses, slums, some of the scariest places that you only see on TV.

Soon it turned into how many men he could get to have sex with me. There were times when I would black out because the fear and pain was so intense. I would be slapped around, kicked, and spat on. I was in a living hell. Every day I woke up wondering if this was my last.

Those three years felt like an eternity. On Christmas Day, 2006, I was literally at rock bottom. My sister called me and I locked myself in the bathroom. She said she felt she needed to call me and tell me to just get out of there. I told her just a little of what was going on. I hid all of this very well. No one knew. I was too ashamed for anyone to know.

I was at one of his relative's homes and my sister told me when I got home to pack up just the necessities and get out. On the way home, he had to stop and meet someone. I knew it was for drugs. When we got home, he went in to the bathroom and snorted it. I was shaking, I knew I had to get out but was afraid he'd kill me. I prayed and asked God for help. I didn't feel like I deserved help but at that moment, I needed it.

He came out of the bathroom and passed out cold on the bed. It was now or never. I quickly got together what I could and threw it in my car. I ran back in to get a few more things and he was standing there and he was mad.

He grabbed me and threw me against the wall. I thought this was it, my family would lose me on Christmas Day. How horrible that would be, they didn't deserve that. He pulled his arm back and was about to punch me. I screamed at the top of my lungs, 'GET OFF ME!' I'd never stood up to him before. The look of shock on his face was clear. He pushed me to the ground and passed back out. I grabbed my keys and ran. I got into my car and as soon as I sat down, my phone rang. It was my dad.

My sister had called him and told him what was going on.

He said, 'Jodi, we love you ... please come home now.' I told him that I was leaving right then. During that two-hour drive home, my

35

mum, Dad, and little sister passed the phone back and forth between them, talking to me the whole way.

Christmas Day 2006 I got my life back.

It wasn't an easy road. I went through a pretty bad depression. I slept on and off for about a month, before I went and looked for a job. But I did it, I got back on my feet and lived!

One year to the day, December 25, 2007, I got engaged to my now husband. It was hard to tell him all I had been through. I still have bad days, I have flash backs and nightmares, but he is there for me and I love him to pieces.

My heart is now full of love and hope. I want to help women who are there or have been where I've been. I want to be a light. I want to be fearless and let them know there is hope and they can be fearless!!!

I want to say with them, 'NO MORE!'

I WILL FIGHT AGAINST DOMESTIC VIOLENCE!

LINDSEY

So, my story begins in November 1995. I worked in a pub on the Wirral. I was a young, single girl of nineteen, not really looking for a relationship and just getting on with life day to day, working, and occasionally going out with friends and spending time with family.

Then, one night, a guy I will call David, came into the pub, not particularly good looking but seemed quite nice and polite when I was serving him and his friends drinks. They stayed all evening and, being the only barmaid on that night, I was on the receiving end of their flirty banter all evening, which I found quite funny and I was flattered by some of the attention. David was very charming and asked me out for a drink and I thought, *why not, it could be fun*. Before I knew it, a whirl-wind romance of flattery and little presents, he moved into my flat within a matter of weeks, we got engaged and set a date to be married in April of the following year, 1996.

Everything went well in this period, we were spending all our time together and he would come into the pub every shift I worked, we went everywhere together. We were never away from each other, this, to me, was what I thought love was really like ... We got married and very quickly became pregnant with a planned pregnancy ... and here I really began to see things were not as normal as I thought they should be ...

Around people, David was very charming and funny. He liked a drink and worked as a chef, he seemed to change jobs a lot but he always said it was to get more money, better hours etc. ... yet he never seemed to have more money or better hours. Behind closed doors, things had started to change. He started to comment more on what I was wearing, I didn't look pretty enough. Why was I wearing my makeup? Was it to impress other men when I worked in the pub? If my friend wanted to come and see me, he would accuse me of having an affair as my friend was male. He made me get rid of all the photos and letters I had received off my friend who was in the army and made me break contact with him, saying if I loved him I wouldn't contact this guy as it upset him. So, being a good wife, I stopped the contact.

As my pregnancy progressed, he started to stay out overnight, saying he was working late and having a few drinks with the lads after work. He stopped paying money towards the bills, saying his wages were being messed up, leaving me to struggle to get everything together for the baby and pay all the bills ... turning to my mum and dad to help, as sometimes I didn't have enough money for food shopping. The times I started to question what he was doing with all his money and telling him that I couldn't do it on my own, he would flair up and get very angry, saying I didn't trust him and asking what kind of wife was I if didn't believe what he said about work messing his wages up? Told me he spent more time in work to try and earn more money. He said I listened to my mum and dad too much and what was the point of me being with him if all I cared about was my family. We had a few arguments and things settled briefly, until one night, he came home after a few drinks and started picking at me, saying I was ugly and ungrateful, I should be happy that I was married and loved with a child on the way when I looked so fat and hideous. Why should he be nice when the baby wasn't his? It was most probably some guy in the pub ... endless abusive comments, day and night, which I thought was normal in marriage ... I tried to defend myself saying I wasn't putting up with the behaviour and the nasty comments and told him that if it didn't stop, I was going to leave ... but instead of being upset by this, he literally got a suitcase, threw all my clothes into it and pushed me towards the stairs, almost forcing me to go down them, saying, 'go on then, run back to mummy and daddy and tell them what a bad husband I am!' ... I tried to go. He blocked me, laughing, saying, 'You are going nowhere with that baby of mine.' He grabbed my arms tight up behind my back and pulled back my hair, saying, 'you can't get along without me, how will you bring a baby up on your own?' Squeezing my fists tightly, I tried to run but he pulled me back and dragged me to the floor and stamped on my hands. Threatened that if I tried to go anywhere, he would take the baby off me as soon as she was born ... He went into my handbag and took my house keys, said I couldn't go anywhere now

38

and he went out, locking the door behind him and leaving me inside. I couldn't get out until he came home that night. That evening, I didn't speak to him. I went to bed and he came up. I had my back to him and he tried to cuddle in, like nothing had happened but I pulled away and he flipped. The anger on his face as he pulled me over on to my back asking how dare I pull away when he was trying to show me he was sorry and as a wife I should do as he said ... so I wriggled to pull away – at this point I was seven months pregnant – he was pinning my arms down to keep me still and sitting on my legs, he tried to learn over to kiss me, so I kept moving and bucking my legs, trying to get him off .... it didn't work ... he said I should do what a wife should do with her husband in bed and he would do it anyway ... I tried to get off the bed, he pinned me down harder and forced himself into me ... he kept going, the whole time I cried ... when he finished, he just turned over and went to sleep.

The next day I couldn't speak to him or look at him. I went to work and came home to a beautiful, big bunch of flowers with *I love you* on. I walked past them. They couldn't fix what he had done. When he came home from work and saw that the flowers hadn't been touched, it set him off again. How selfish was I not to accept the flowers he had bought to cheer me up? He was in my face, raging. I had learnt to stand still and not react at this. He went on and on for about ten mins, and then sat down. After that, the sexual side of things didn't happen again or the hurting me physically because he realised it left marks. People had seen the bruises and heard the rows. He was learning to be more careful. We went through many more physical assaults.

I had a little girl and for a while, everything settled down and we seemed happy. I thought things were getting better. But slowly, again, money stopped coming home, he was drinking and gambling more, I had lost contact with all my friends. I only got to see my mum and dad, and he was usually with me. I worked and looked after the baby. He worked and drank, left everything to me. His money was his to do with as he wished he said, I was becoming a nag and why should he pay for a baby that most probably wasn't his? Since being pregnant, why would a man want me? I was lucky I still had him. By this time, I felt isolated and alone and ashamed. I hid everything from everyone. Covered up all the money issues but Mum and Dad knew that something was up; I denied it all … I lost a lot of weight. I developed bulimia from trying to hide all the worry and stress. My confident, bubbly nature had gone. I became quiet and withdrawn. I was alone. I didn't feel I could tell anyone. So, life carried on. An endless circle of being told how bad I was, threats to take my baby if I didn't do as I was told, hardly any access to money as he wouldn't give me any, only my wages to cover the bills. I had no friends, no life …

Then it changed. He became a charmer again, he was nice for three to four months – he settled and it was as though the worst was behind us. We moved and bought a house. Everything seemed okay and we chose to have another baby. Sex was back on the menu but it wasn't loving. It was still 'going through the motions', but I wanted a brother or sister for my daughter and I thought things would be okay. Behind the scenes, it turns out he was happy as, unknown to me, he was seeing someone else.

We were settled in our new house, my second daughter was six weeks from being born, the emotional mind games had well and truly returned but again, I was trapped in a world of fear and silence and there was no one I could turn to. Something snapped inside me one night when he was kicking off again, he went to kick me in the stomach while pregnant … I pulled a knife out of the drawer and held it in front of me and said, 'If you touch this baby it will be the last thing you do!' He laughed and said I wouldn't touch him, I just screamed at him to get out of my way.

He got my daughter and said, 'You won't touch me when I have her, you will not do anything because if I go, she goes with me.' I backed down. The abuse from then on became every few days. Kicks in the legs, stomps on my upper arms.

When baby number two was born, he wanted sex. I had given birth three days before and baby was in the cot at side of me. I was tired and sore. He wanted what he wanted but I said no so he pinned me down and took what he wanted. I cried and cried and kicked him off the bed, he dragged the mattress off with me on it and threw it against the wall, knocking the baby's cot in the process, luckily just on the edge and she was okay. He then dragged me up by my hair and pushed me back to the ground, belting my head on the skirting board my head spun and the room went white. I passed out.

I woke up on the sofa with the baby's crib next to me, my eldest daughter had slept through it all. When I went to check on her, he was sitting in front of her nursery and said 'You ain't going in … you have no chance, you are not getting near that child.' I tried to drag him out, I didn't want him anywhere near her. He wouldn't go so with my little baby, I ran to a local church I had started to attend just to get away from him and for the first time, I told them of this episode, of the abuse, not all the details, just as if it was a row. She took me the police and I made a complaint and they rung him to tell him to behave and to let me see to my daughter. He did and he promised to get help and never do it again. He went to the doctors and told me they said he had anger issues and would see a counsellor. I believed him. He lied. Within weeks, the emotional abuse was back, all the time. Money was none existent for me and the children. My mum and dad were paying for food and nappies but still I hid what was going on. After a few months, two more violent attacks came about, not long before my youngest daughter's first birthday and christening.

These two attacks ending up being the best two things to happen to me because they started to make me realise enough was enough. The worm was finally turning. My ex had come in after a few drinks and I was cross, asked why he could do that but not support his family? He went nuts, for the first time ever he assaulted me in front of our daughters, who now were two and a half and one. He kicked me in the legs with steel-toe-capped boots on, he dragged me into the hall and closed the living room door where the girls played on the floor. He pinned me down, banging my head on the floor and he kept pouring jugs of water down my throat, making me choke. After a few minutes he just got up, threw a towel at me and went to our daughters, playing at being a wonderful daddy. I snapped inside, I decided I needed to get him out, but I knew it would take time.

I had become good friends with the lady next door, Sue. She came around when he went to work the next day and said that she had been hearing a lot of what had what had been going on and couldn't keep quiet any longer. She wanted to know what was happening. Finally, I broke down and admitted everything. Sue became my strength, my guardian angel. We talked a lot about when and where and how I could end this nightmare. We went to the police and got my bruises logged but at that time, nothing was done. I said I wanted to get my children out safely. We carried on as normal for about a week while I was trying to make a plan, then one night he came home at three in the morning, smelling of perfume. I was really upset. I asked if he was seeing someone else and he laughed, said, 'As if, but it's your fault if I am.' I cried and said I was going to bed as I was too tired to argue anymore and I had a headache. He grabbed me by the hair and said, 'take these if you have a headache!' he force-fed me fourteen paracetamol tablets and poured a drink down my throat, forcing me to swallow them and then stood up. Luckily the girls were sleeping at their grandparents that night. I begged him to ring an ambulance but he wouldn't, so I did. They came and took me to hospital and asked what I had taken but he was with me. He told them I had got angry and overdosed. They gave me a charcoal solution to throw up all the paracetamol. As the doctors were coming to talk to me, he said I would never see my children again if I told them the truth about what happened, so I told them it was just a reaction to an argument and they let us go home. I was so scared now, I really didn't think there was anything I could do could get out of this mess.

Christmas came and went, nothing was better. I had decided I was going to leave and saw a solicitor, on the quiet, about a divorce. He agreed it was the right thing to do and gave me the number of the Zero Centre in Birkenhead, a place for domestic violence sufferers to get support. I put it in my purse and thought I'd call them at the beginning of the following week as it was my youngest daughters christening that Sunday and her grandparents were to be godparents and everyone was coming.

The day went brilliantly. Then, on the following Tuesday, my world ended. My dad died of a heart attack. This turned out to be final kick I needed. Here I am, my dad is dead, I have two children under the age of three, I am numb with pain and have no emotion to show. I try and talk to my husband but he calls me cold hearted and horrid for not crying, tells me what an awful daughter I was for not being upset. He slaps my face and says, 'You can cry when I do that but you won't for your dad?'

For the first time, I felt the anger I needed to make the change. I wanted him gone; whatever it took …

I went to the Zero Centre, they helped me get a divorce solicitor, who started taking down all the details of the abuse and the divorce proceedings started. I told my mum, a male cousin who I trusted, and my friend next door. We worked out a plan to get him out of the house within a few days, while keeping the kids safe in the process. He came home at three in the morning again, I was awake and he tried to come near me, I went downstairs, he followed, I said I wanted a divorce as I was sick of the violence and the fact that I knew, and had confirmation, he was also seeing someone else. I handed him a bag I had prepared for him with clothes and photos of the children and asked him, politely, to leave. I knew that he was not going to take it lightly but I was prepared for it. I had a phone in my pocket and had told my neighbour that if he kicked off, I would dial from my pocket and she was to ring two numbers: the police and my cousin around the corner. He could get to me to help until the police arrived. So my husband, for the final time, flared up, like I had never seen before. It turned out to be my worst, but final attack. I was pulled everywhere, banged into everything, kicked, and punched but this time … I fought back.

I punched, I kicked, I screamed. Anything to get him away from me until he pinned me down and tried to suffocate me with a pillow over my mouth. I somehow managed to dial the number on the mobile, just by hitting the 'one' button I had programmed for speed dial. My neighbour had a key to let the police and my cousin in. She rang them both and my cousin turned up, the door flew open just as my husband belted up the stairs to get the kids to take them from me. My cousin went up the stairs after him but David jumped over part of the stairs, past my cousin, and ran out of the house. Up the street. The police pulled up and looked for him but couldn't find him. He was gone and I was free.

Unlike now, there was no automatic way the police could charge and punish abusers. At the time, I had a restraint put in place to keep him away from me but he was gone. I got him out with the help of my guardian angels.

I took back the control and my kids never remembered any of it. I didn't have him charged as, at the time, I was worried about the kids seeing their dad. I wish I had now if I'm honest but at the same time, my children never felt I stopped them seeing their dad and he chose not to bother with them. So, he was gone, life had to go on, the Zero Centre helped me with a course called the Venus Programme, which helped me to empower myself again. I lost my house but moved closer to my mum for a while, got a new job, new home, and started therapy for my eating disorder. Domestic abuse counselling helped too. I threw myself into everything, slowly coming to terms with things in my own way. I looked pretty, I lost weight, made friends, but it was all still hard. I had nightmares and panic attacks but I fought against it all. I was getting me back.

After three years, I met someone else who treated me like a princess, except he was genuine. In time, he helped heal some of my bruises and held me through the nightmares. We got married, had a son, and he brought my daughters up as his. He was the best dad the kids could have, sadly we divorced two years later, I still hadn't quite dealt with the past. We parted on brilliant terms, I am godmother to his children in his new relationship. We remain close, his girlfriend is family to me. A truly positive happy ending to a second marriage breakdown but I never regretted that second marriage as it was all part of my healing process.

Over time, I went back for more counselling and started training my mind in positive thinking. I came off anti-depressants, after over ten years, I had a few fun relationships in between but I stayed single to find myself, finally and properly.

Here I am now, a new person; qualified as a teaching assistant working in a school I love, with some fabulous, wonderful friends who are like family and I have brought my children up in the best home I could give them. But most of all, I am happy. I like me, I am confident. In control of my own life, single through choice, because I don't feel the need to be in a relationship now. I have a totally open heart to meeting someone if they come along, except this time, no ghosts of the past to interfere with it. The kids came through things happy. I have no anger or bitterness. Yes, I will always have flashbacks, it never truly leaves you but it just becomes a part of you that you choose to let go. It no longer consumes me. I am happy.

And my abuser? Well he went on to do it several more times, my only regret is I should have had him charged at the time, but now he has lost everything and I have everything and I have, last year, even made my peace. I cannot forgive and forget, but I can stop it bothering me. I even gave him a hug at a family funeral recently, with no feeling, other than that of empowerment, that I could hug and no longer be held by the past. In a way, it's because of him I feel so happy today, because that final attack made me fight back and find out who I was … I truly believe we go through such negative things in life to make us stronger and grow into who we become. I started martial arts classes where I met my closest friends, who are my extended family now. I made wonderful friends at church, trained for a new career, and feel truly blessed in life. Out of the darkness came a light and I shine on. I could write more, in detail, but it's a story that could go on for a life time but now I'll stop, because now is what matters.

LIESL

See, I don't know how it began because I think it was such a drip, drip, drip, a gradual process. We ended up conditioning each other. The earliest things that I remember being an issue were his insecurities about me and other men and whether they were interested in me and whether I was interested in them. My assurances that I wasn't and that it was ridiculous, meant nothing because he knows what men are like. Then every place that I worked, there would be a male colleague and I always got on with them. When I was at college I always had more male friends than female, that's always been the case. So, I would make friends and I would talk about them, I was certain I would talk about them all the same but he said I would talk about the men more, which was probably just what he was focussing on more than anything. But they were good friends and they probably were flirty and fun because that's how I am and that's what he loved about me to start with and to be honest it's probably because I flirted with him.

But then there would be the suggestions that that was inappropriate, that actually, there was more going on ... there never was ... and I started justifying myself all the time. Then I started watching what I was saying about these people, that then led to watching what I was saying about everything else that I was doing, of course being careful about what I was wearing because if I was wearing something lower or shorter than normal it was because I must be meeting somebody and this went on and on and on.

And then I had my dalliance. And from then on, that was it, everything that I did was, just, everything was my fault and it got to the stage where I was just watching everything, I was so in control of myself; what I was saying, what I was doing, where I was going, who with, what I was wearing, what I was telling him about it afterwards, trying to avoid the telling off. And it wasn't even that he would necessarily shout, I would just have this anxiety that he was going to ... kick off.

We'd be going to the cinema and I'd choose where we were sitting and it was never good enough – it wasn't the right seat, it was too far to the left or to the right or too far back or what have you, and it got to the stage where we would go to the cinema and I refused to choose where the seat was because it was easier to say, 'You know what, I don't care where we're sitting. I wanna enjoy the film, you choose.' Because that would avoid that sort of anxiety inducing constant negativity, I suppose, just constant negativity that it was all my fault. It was all encompassing, it was every part of life. And after we separated, well, in fact, I after I knew we were separating, I felt, it was a good day, you know how you walk with a bounce sometimes with a half-smile on your face, and I was walking through Birmingham train station and I bounced past people and there were momentary glances that you'll have when you've got this half-smile on your face and you might get a half-smile back and I'm walking up, striding along the street and it's all great, everything is great and I realise that was the first time I was walking through a crowd with my eyes looking up because I had got into the habit of looking down, whether I was with him or not, so I could never get accused of looking at another man.

I can still picture that, I can picture some of the people I saw; these formative moments where I thought this is how bad it got. I wasn't me, I couldn't be me.

There was one time, when my son went missing in a shop, there was me and my mum in the Early Learning Centre and we went to show him something and he'd gone. He wasn't there, he'd wandered out, it was only in the town centre here so it was indoors and he wasn't gone for long and we went to the information centre and we got there just as some other woman handed him over as a lost child. My mum burst into tears of relief and I realised that at no point through the whole process from realising he was missing till we found him, at no point did I feel any emotion. I didn't feel fear. I didn't feel concern. I didn't feel worry. I didn't feel relief. Absolutely nothing. I had deadened all of my emotional responses because I had to be in so much control of everything that I was feeling that I just wasn't me anymore. So that's what it got to, but how it got there …

I felt resentful about the way he would put pressure on me about my relationships with men and other people, I wasn't happy, I knew it was unfair, I had never done anything that deserved it, not that anyone ever deserves it but I had never done anything to make him doubt how I felt about him and the relationship, there had never – until my dalliance – there had never been any suggestion that these guys I was working with, were anything other than work colleagues. I was occasionally out with them socially but as a work colleague, that was it.

So, I felt a frustration, but he couldn't see that. I felt hurt that he didn't trust me, but again, it would be justified … as in, I'd think *oh okay it's fine, he loves me so what if he's a bit possessive and you know what, I'd probably be a bit upset if I saw him flirt with somebody* and so I totally justified it, whilst at the same maintaining a level of frustration and resentment that this wasn't me, but I didn't overly challenge it, I'm sure I probably did challenge it sometimes, I can't remember, there will have a been a half-hearted affair or he would have justified it some way that sounded feasible and reasonable at the time. And probably the first time, it was such a minor thing that his response probably did seem reasonable and the next time it would have grown on that, but because you've accepted the first one, you're giving him a little bit of a start so from beginning to end, it's a huge impact, but each time, not really noticing.

I can't think that I ever really challenged him, more I just put up with it and I accepted it, like *oh here we go again, it's fine.*

We did go to counselling at one point and I did say that I didn't think that I was me and that I was smothering everything, this was half way through the relationship, and even in the counselling she would say, 'You want this marriage to work, what are you going to do? How are you going to put it right? You had a dalliance, this is your fault.' And I'm sure the counsellor didn't intend for that but that is exactly what happened and it was all again, justifying his control, without calling it control. 'It's not control, Lisle, it's you just doing what you can to make the marriage work.'

I had known for quite a while that he was abusive and I knew that I was never bloody gonna to do anything about it, we had kids, it was scary. I was working an hour away from home, long hours in a law firm and my salary from that wouldn't have been enough to get somewhere and be able to have the kids. If I was working full-time, how was that going to work with the kids? So, there was the whole practicalities of it, I didn't know what the dynamics of it could be, so it was always, when the kids have grown up ... eventually ... I knew I wasn't happy, I knew it wasn't working, it wasn't worth fighting for, the potential for feeling guilt was also quite strong. I didn't want to be the one to blame. You know, I'm the one that brings it to an end and that's my fault and I didn't want that on my head.

And then yes, I discovered he had an affair but it was still eight months before I said enough is enough, when I went out with Patrick that night and I realised that I still couldn't go out without feeling anxious, I was still watching the time, I was still home at half past nine from a night out for god's sake. I still had to think about what I was going to say to him when I got back, what am I gonna tell him? What am I not gonna tell him? What if he finds out? What if he's bugged my phone? What if he knows all of this and is just waiting to see if what I say catches me out? What if I've worn something and the buttons are too low? The constant what if – watching myself was exhausting and it was just that, being able to finally verbalise, to myself more than anything, over that two-week period before the counselling, I tried building on what I was saying without fear of any sort of reaction.

I think, without the affair ... I needed that drive ...

I didn't have any family or friends during this relationship who I confided in and who were able to say that the behaviour was unhealthy. Mum and Dad, knowing what they know now, are absolutely horrified that they didn't know and erm, they can see a difference in me but I was with him from when I was twenty-one, that was most of my adult life so as far as they knew, that was who I was and they didn't know that it wasn't right. Now they know, Dad can see that I'm totally different.

Friends, I spoke to them about him, yeah, they knew that I wasn't happy, that I had to watch what I was saying, where I was going, they knew that I wasn't often going out with them, and I think one or two of knew. There was one good friend of mine who was aware of it and used to tell me that it was ridiculous. No one ever told me that I should get out, nobody ever thought that, they just thought, well, she's not allowed to do something, he's being unfair – this is ridiculous, it was that sort of thing. And then when it got towards when I'd made the decision to go, and there were more reactions from him or more things came out, the DNA test thing and things like that, there was absolute outrage from my friends on my behalf. And I still couldn't feel it, I squashed them. I'd think really? *You're talking about me here?* And they were absolutely incensed.

There was this one night when I had gone out again and we had already said that we were separating, and he was unhappy with the fact that I had gone out, so he packed all the room up into bags and suitcases and put them on the porch and then rang me while I was out to say it's all on the porch, don't come back. So, I had to go, that evening, because I had nowhere else to go, I think at that point I had the place I was moving in to lined up, but that night I go and sit and capitulate and yes, you're absolutely right, I was outrageous and I knew I was watching myself and I knew what I was doing, I knew what he was doing at this point, but I was learning to see. And he was making little comments that would have passed me by but obviously would have gone in, but I wouldn't have noticed them. But on that occasion, there was a voice in the back of my head that would be saying, 'oh well played him – how subtle, well done.' But I was seeing it now, I was allowing it because it served a purpose till I could get out.

But that night, when my two friends were with me, they had to speak to him to make sure I was okay to stop there and just be there as a third party.

I think I am still very tightly in control, although I say that, I wonder whether most of that is just the trust issue that prevents me feeling too much, you know, I'm seeing someone, it's a new relationship, it's lovely, I'm totally smitten but there's still a part of me that says, 'hold back, don't totally connect to this, don't totally invest because you've had a bad time.'

I don't know whether that's my control of my emotions or whether that's just not trusting, or whether they're so bloody totally integrated it's the same thing and I think there is still an element of … it's a survival mechanism … when something bad happens, I don't necessarily immediately feel bad. There's part of me aware that I'm feeling nothing and I have absolutely screamed at myself in my head, 'Feel this! How dare you not feel this upsetting thing that is happening?' I still don't know that I ever will. There are other emotions that I do feel, it's not completely dead, it was, it is coming back ... so who knows? Maybe it will ... it's mostly the negative stuff that I don't let myself feel. So actually, if I don't feel shit, I'm happy with that. But you're supposed to feel shit about some things, but it does bring in a practicality. When my son went missing in the town centre and I didn't feel fear or what have you, I went totally into practical mode ... where do I get him? There was no panic, all calm ... so it's not all bad.

I don't know when it started coming back. I suppose just that walk through the train station actually, I was feeling good that day. That was me, allowing myself to express the fact that I was feeling good and I hadn't even left at that point. I'd said I was separated, I'd said I wanted a divorce.

The majority of the relationship was negative, which was so normal, I stopped responding to negatives. So now I know I can be happy, I am hoping that will come back in allowing me to love fully. And trust, trust is a big thing, it is a requirement, it is a huge thing, it is there and it is growing, but I think that's got to be ... you know – trust grows doesn't it.

There's this thing, I tell everyone about ...

So, imagine a field, there's this high grass, waist high grass and you're at point X. The truth, or the trust, is at point A but the grass is really high and it's hard to get there. So, if you want to get there it's hard work, you have to trample the grass down, whereas at point B, is the distrust, which is well worn, there's a path there. So, by default, that's where you go because it's easier; I quite trust, I can see the trust over there, but actually, this path is easier. And the building trust thing is the gradual going to point A, trampling down the grass, making a new path and at the same time, at point B where there is no trust, the grass is growing, making that harder and you're forging a new path but it takes time and you have to build on it every time. It works with trust, it works with truth as well.

That was told to me in the context of not being able to tell my husband what I'd been doing in the day, I couldn't tell the truth because it was easier just to lie and not deal with the fall out. I had to gradually be telling the truth more and more and work on that new path and allow the old path of not telling the truth, to wear away. That would work in a normal, healthy relationship, however, in an abusive relationship, as I'm trying to make this path and trying to grow the grass on this other path, he's the one trampling over the new path and cutting down that grass because of course, every time I was caught out, that was something else he could use as ammunition against me. I say that like it was really conscious but I don't know, I can't decide if it was.

When I say, 'caught out' ... I was quite a good girl! I didn't do anything bad to be honest, I don't even recall a particular occasion where I was caught out, but that night I went out with a certain man, I was terrified of saying he wasn't here and him saying, 'yes he was and you lied.' The fall out would be that much greater, I knew that, now I don't know where I've learnt that from there must have been occasions where I have lied and got caught out, I suppose with my dalliance, and that was an example of me not telling the truth and then the truth sort of came out and the fall out was so much worse but it was never anything that I had done, I didn't do anything! And I was still trying to justify this, even now. I didn't do anything. It was so uncalled for.

I had my truth and I had to deal with his truth; which was that I was fucking everyone nearby. In my job, I am used to disagreeing with people and having arguments and having different opinions, and that's okay. I can still have my say and they'll have their say and we disagree but dealing with him, I could never persuade him to my way of thinking, that was never going to happen but he was absolutely adamant that I was to agree with him. That I would see things his way, that his way was the right way. And because I disagreed with him, I was wrong. He couldn't conceive with the possibility that we both had opinions that could still fit together and it not really matter that we disagree. That was exhausting actually.

I have found that I have got more willing to confront people that I disagree with, people that I think are being unfair. My son was being bullied at school, actually, he wasn't, the other kid's dad accused my son of being the bully and I rang him up and said, 'Let's go for a pint and sort this out.' I didn't expect him to agree with me, he thinks his kid's being bullied and he doesn't know. I think that my son is not bullying but I don't know, I'm not there at the occasion, so there's room for both of us to be wrong here. I recognised that and I expected him to be the same way. So, I thought let's get you a pint and we'll talk it out, we'll figure out how we're going to deal with the kids and teach them how to deal with the dispute. Well, he wasn't having that, I was a complete idiot for believing my son but he couldn't see the irony of the fact that he was doing the same and he did tell me I don't want anything to do with you or your son, so no, he wouldn't come to the pub with me. I was a liar, I can still hear the venom in his words. For one of the few times where I've had a personal … where I've had to deal with it and not delegate it to someone else like my ex, I dealt with it, and I responded and it didn't end particularly well but I held my ground and then I hung up and I burst into tears because I couldn't yet cope with the stress that comes with a confrontation. Because actually, a confrontation is stressful at some level and some of us are better at dealing with that than others and I was not yet in a position where I could. But I would always delegate things like that to my ex. Things like going on holiday and signing in at the hotel, I have no idea what I'm doing; do they need the passports or not? I have no idea. And if I had of done it, I wouldn't do it quick enough or I would have gotten it wrong somehow, it was easier to let him do it. I delegated so much.

I went on holiday in March with my new partner and they were more wussy than me, I got forced into being the organiser, I was the one who booked us into the hotel, I was the one who bartered on the market, I'd never bartered in my life! I'd never been brave enough but my friend wanted a handbag and she wasn't going to do it so I had to barter and it was fun, it was okay, I was shit at it and she still had to pay over the odds but I attempted it. And it was because I was forced in to it when previously, my ex would do it. And as a result of that, I realised that actually I can do that whereas before, my ex was quite happy for me to think that I couldn't and that made him feel like he was the big man and I was the little lady and I couldn't possibly do this to reinforce the hierarchy.

But no more.

My life now is all good really. I have a new relationship which is lovely. I'm loving it. I'm very tentative, moving at a snail's pace, eighteen-year-old me would have been like, 'what? Just move on!' It's slow, it's so slow that it even frustrates me but I'm also the one who sabotages any progress. I've become aware of that this weekend. But it's good. I am terrified of it now progressing because until now, I could genuinely say to my ex – no I'm not seeing anyone, the last person I had sex with was you. Not that I'm ever going to say that, but the point is that he felt that I was to blame for having a relationship with my friend when I wasn't, now I am having a relationship with that friend, it's just going to justify everything that he said about that thing, and I hate that.

So, the relationship's good, work's good, the arrangements with the kids are being sorted out, is sorted out, we had that issue with him making the death threats and my response to that, which was dreadful, but then I recovered and strengthened my position as a result of telling him how it was and he's behaved generally since then. There have been issues and arguments but it's mostly like when the kids have to go to the dentist, he was taking them and he took them out of school early but it was a horrendous morning, we were late to school, the kids hadn't brushed their teeth, I had been oblivious to this, we'd rushed in to school, they were late already. My ex picks them up and their teeth are mucky. So, I get no end of text messages about how outrageous this is, how it's just basic stuff. And part of me was just reading these text messages and thinking, yeah, whatever. But a big part of me had that anxious feeling in my belly that I was in the wrong again and he was probably justified, which I hate, but in the scheme of things, you were going to get them to clean their teeth before the dentist weren't you? So, it was no big thing, but it was another example ... he would tell the kids things about his new relationship that I think is inappropriate, I've commented that my son has told me he has seen his dad in bed with another woman and that he just ought to be careful with what they see and of course it got turned around to ask if the kids knew I was sharing a bed with my new partner. He said he'd spoken to our son about it and I thought, why would you? He's spoken to me in confidence and I'm trying to help him out by not destroying the relationship with your kids, and I'm trying to help you out with this and you talk to him about it and make it into a big thing. Of course, my son denies saying anything because he can't talk to his dad about any of that sort of stuff, and you know, saying, 'Hey, Dad, I saw you in bed with someone and I didn't like it.' He's ten, so then I get a text message saying that he is denying it so I don't know if he's lying or you're recording calls and trying to set me up. What?! It's little things like that which still have the impact.

My car broke down when I was visiting family in the north-east of England and I had the kids with me and we had to get home. My dad took us half way and my ex picked us up. Which was okay, we were okay enough that we could spend two and half hours in a car together. The interesting thing for me was that we were late setting off and I knew we would be late getting to the meeting point and my dad said I should send a message. So, I sent the message saying we were running a bit late but I'll keep you posted. I couldn't bring myself to say about half an hour late, so, I got a reply asking how late, and I started feeling anxious. I'm two hours away from him, I've got my dad there as support, we're talking about me letting him, quite politely, know that we were going to be late to a meeting by about half an hour because I thought it was going to be … So, I put about fifteen minutes but we're in traffic, pathing the way for saying this was why we were even more late. But he ended up getting there half an hour early so he's sat there for an hour. Which was okay, I did get a number of text messages saying bloody hell, there's been road works all the way and all the negativity that comes with that. But that wasn't necessarily then directed at me but then I had chosen where we were going to meet therefore, it was my fault he had to get through the road works to get there. But it wasn't that he was having a go at me for the roadworks, but nevertheless, I'm conditioned to take on that control.

So, there's little things like that that still get to me. I'm worried about developing my relationship with my new partner because at some point, I'm going to have to tell my ex.

We've talked about having kids, I'd love to have another kid, if I'm going to, I better hurry up because I'm forty-one. It's only gonna happen in the next couple of years or not at all. Which means we need to think about this, we need to make this relationship quite solid. But that means telling my ex. And that terrifies me. I don't know what he would do, I don't how he would do it, I don't know whether it would actually have an effect but I haven't yet got to the stage of indifference that I really want to be at, where I don't care about what his response is but he still does get that response. It isn't any of his business.

I would be so happy if this new relationship developed into something special, I've always wanted three kids, I used to joke with my ex that I wanted three children, he wanted three too but he already one so I was never going to be able to catch up, which seemed a bit unfair at the time. I never actually thought it would happen! And now I've got the opportunity to be able to do it, as and when I'm ready to.

NICKI MURPHY

Amidst the sounds of animals, a girl stood and realised that, for the first time in her life, things were perhaps not as they should be. She loved her life and those around her, all but one. The one she had feared for so many years, who drove her waking thoughts and insecurities, maligning her in every way possible, making her believe things were not as others told her.

For as long as she could remember she had believed that she was fat, ugly, and would never amount to anything. Oh yes – she had rebelled – only to be told she was argumentative, disruptive, unruly, and loud.

At this point, amongst the stillness, she realised that none of this was true. Was it?

Friends and others had made comments without prompt that she was calm and supportive, passive, and quiet. How could she believe anything else? Her head wanted to explode as the memories overcame her.

A life of insecurity, questioning who and what she was; a life of standing back and wishing. Wishing that the one person who had stood beside her and given her confidence was still there. Thankfully, his presence lingered and she now began to think of him often, the things he would say about the various situations she found herself in. Such as dealing with her abuser, something she had little choice about because of who they are.

In any other relationship, she was sure they would have divorced or been reported to the police, to be dealt with by the law but in her case, that wasn't possible as she was a child no longer, but an adult. A fact she had to remember. A fact her counsellor went over with her time and again. Not a child to be told what she could and couldn't do, how she should behave, what she should choose and wear.

An adult. Really? The years she had been beholden to this person, requiring their support before every decision and then even when she felt rebellious, would worry over what would be said … or done. She wasn't a stranger to violence and re-lived those painful times, time and again.

This power had held her back but now she finally realised it was weakening and like the chrysalis, she was beginning to feel her wings. They were far from unfurling but she could feel the breeze she needed to take her to a different place. One where she could be herself and not have to think anymore. A world away from the pain she had suffered for so many years.

In the stillness, she gazed at her animals, they were her comfort. It was to them she always turned when she had no one else, when she'd been told she was in the wrong. Now she realised this was no longer true. No one can make you 'feel'.

There is a choice, there is help, and there is hope.

Reap what you sow.

She certainly hoped so.

BIANCA

I was twenty-three and he was a lot older; a bad boy who I thought I could tame. He showed controlling signs from very early on, although I didn't see it straight away. When he deleted every male (family included) from my Facebook, that was when I thought it was a little too much. He chose who I would and wouldn't see, which became a lot easier for him as no one wanted to see me while I was with him, not even my family. They really disliked him.

I fell pregnant and moved away from everyone, having only him and my young son. I didn't know anyone in the new area. He controlled money, I had a set amount for shopping and that was it. He would drink away any other money I had. He had a very short temper and would explode at anything.

The night that ended everything for me, my son had gone to the toilet for a wee; he came back in to me and then ran back out to the bathroom saying he needed a number two. He started to shout, saying my son was thick for not doing both at the same time, he threw his tea across the room. I sorted my son and put him in his room, when I went back downstairs, he grabbed me and put a knife to my pregnant stomach and said he was going to give me an abortion. I managed to get out of his way after he threw me to the floor. I went and got my son and left.

I rang the only lady I had come to know in the area and she came to pick us up, we stayed that night at her house. The next day, after dropping our children at nursery, my friend and her husband came home with me. My house had been trashed, the front door had been kicked in, there was urine all over the floors downstairs and my underwear was ripped up and scattered around the house. There was a photograph of me and my son on the floor, with an apology on the back and the usual *I love you* and *can't live without you*. Next the photo was a couple of empty tablet packets.

I contacted the police and received a lot of support from them and the domestic violence team. They helped house me and made me feel safe in my new home with a panic alarm and extra locks.

At the time, I felt extremely stupid that I didn't listen to people when they told me how it would end. I was ashamed I allowed myself to be treated that way. I had, by this point, believed what he told me, I was useless, stupid, ugly inside and out, and no one other than him would ever want me.

I haven't heard from him in six years, I found everything was a struggle to begin with, especially the mental abuse, but now I can say I'm okay and mean it!

I'm now in a happy, stable relationship and we are expecting baby number four! We are all happy and healthy.

SUSAN HOPCROFT

S: It began when my mum died. She was a salvationist, and I tried to be like her – my first abuser, who was an alcoholic, sniffed glue, all sorts of problems with him, mental as well as other issues, I tried to help him and invited him in to my life. My idea at that point was *I'm going to change him*. Well, instead of changing him, he ended up beating me, hitting me, dragging me in to a life with drugs … I started using cannabis and speed because that's what he was doing as well … I went around with him and his mates – he used to rape me, batter me.

I had to put my eldest son in care because I couldn't look after him because at that point I was a mess … I then, after a while had been battered and abused and the police kept moving me because I kept going to them for help and they kept moving me but he kept following me so I was in this circle … in the end, I got gang raped by him and five of his mates and I was taken to hospital because I was really badly hurt and at that point, the police actually said to me, 'We're going to move you out of London to a different area.' And I moved – I was pregnant and, at that time, I had my son back with me – up to Leeds to start a new life.

And we did … for a while.

Then my daughter was born … with many problems, she still has health problems, then basically, after a while, I got lonely 'cause living on your own is not good, it takes a lot to actually get out of that circle of not being able to live on your own. So, I had lots of boyfriends but none of them were much good. Finally, I got with another guy and he was fine. Because of the abuse I'd ended up, for the first time, in a wheelchair and his idea was that while I was in a wheelchair, I was controllable, so even though there was no actual physical abuse with him, it was emotional abuse – I wasn't able to get up and do what I wanted to do, I had to rely on him.

I decided one day that this was not my life anymore and I started trying to get out a bit and walk a bit, go on special courses that actually helped me walk, I had a couple of operations which solved some of my issues. But then I wasn't any good anymore and he pushed me down the stairs, hoping that he would keep in a wheelchair. But he didn't and I didn't actually leave him, he actually left me because another guy at that point started hanging around, he was an Italian, and I though he was everything I wanted … he was a strong man, he didn't seem like he was abusive, in fact, he seemed perfect in lots and lots of ways but within about two weeks of him moving in, I started to realise he wasn't actually that perfect.

He was very controlling. His idea of life was the mafia, so as a woman, I had to wear long skirts or trousers, I wasn't allowed to show anything above my ankles, that was not allowed. My daughter was very controlled too and so I went to my best friend and she actually took my daughter to live with her.

I had to pick him up and drive him where he said, even though I didn't have a driving license at the time, I only had a provisional, but that didn't count and I would always have to drive around a specific block to make sure there was no police on the estate but it was really silly because if there were police on the estate, they were gonna pull us because I didn't have a license, but that didn't enter into his thoughts.

At that time, my son was eighteen and he had just found himself a flat on this particular estate and he knew this guy, Terry. By this time, I was back on the drugs in a big way. I used to do a lot of drugs especially speed, amphetamine, because I was always fat and this guy always called me fat and I had to lose weight and the only way of losing weight was to do drugs – so Terry kinda entered in my life because he could see that my life wasn't good but when I met him, he was already going back to prison … he had a record, he'd done armed robbery, burglary of banks when he was twenty-one. But he didn't seem a bad guy, he seemed a caring guy and I actually went to visit him in prison and yeah, he seemed all right.

When he came out of prison, we kinda got together but soon I realised he wasn't so good either because you couldn't do anything or say anything without him saying so and then the abuse started. If he was in a mood with me he'd chuck me out of the flat and I'd have to spend the night in the car, but I still stuck with him and then the hitting started and the back on the glue started. I watched him one day have an argument with this one guy and he picked this guy up by the throat and that scared me. Then he started getting really sexual with me; he wanted sex but he wanted it his way and no other way but he wouldn't sleep in the same bed as me so it was very much like I was his property. I couldn't wear anything unless he approved of it and quite often, in the morning, he'd come in and get the clothes out and say, 'That's what you're wearing today.'

So that carried on for a while and I was getting deeper and deeper in this *I can't escape mode*, and that's the best way to say it, it's like you want to leave but you can't leave. You want to be free but you can't be free.

Int: How did you feel through those relationships then?

S: I wasn't worthy, I wasn't liked, I wasn't wanted. That's what my life was all about. You don't feel like you're ever gonna find anybody else, you never feel like you're gonna be free, you never feel that you can go to sleep at night and not have someone come in and for no reason other because you're asleep, have them throw water over you and he doesn't want you to sleep.

So, I went through five years of that and it got worse. There wasn't ever a time that I could say it got easier and he always said it was my fault and he'd say he was sorry. That was one thing he always used to say, he was sorry, but it was my fault. I spent a couple of weeks in hospital because he battered me that hard that I was in such a state I couldn't even walk ... life was difficult, all his friends bowed down to him, I mean, there was a couple of guys he used to hang around with, they were only young themselves, and if he clicked his fingers, they would turn up really quick, one of them worked as a garage mechanic and even the garage where he worked knew Terry cause he used to take his car there and they used to get everything perfect because they were so frightened of him kicking off ... I mean this was Terry, he was six feet, seven and a half inches tall – massive – had hands like shovels. So, when he hit you, he hit you ... there was no little tap, it was a major deal. And ... life was hard. But I didn't ever think I'd get out of it.

Int: But when you got out of it, how did you feel then?

S: Scared. I mean he did something for me, the only thing I'll say for Terry, because I won't lie about this, the one good thing that Terry did for me was he got me off drugs. He might not have done it the proper way, he smacked the hell out of me, said if I take drugs again he'll beat the hell out of me again and then he gave me a deal, I could have, instead of having the drugs, I could have a glass of Bailey's. So, whenever I felt like I needed the speed or the amphetamines, I could have a glass, I did two weeks cold turkey and he stuck by me and you know, yeah, he did hit me but he got me off drugs and I won't take that away from him, he did that for me but if you look at everything I had to put with, I think I paid him back basically.

He even did a Christmas for me, because my daughter ended up with my best friend, and social services got involved, I could only see my daughter once a month and that was under my friend's supervision. So, basically, just before Christmas, I always got a visit with my daughter so Terry made the arrangement that my son would come down from Leeds, or Hull because my son lived in Hull then, with his girlfriend and her two children, and my daughter would come from Milton Keynes and we had a Christmas together. He cooked the dinner and everything for us and it was lovely. But even at the end of that he had to put his stamp on it and he refused to take my son and his girlfriend back to the station – I think it was one of their children didn't respect that the food was cooked and he had to wait until Terry said he could eat the food. So therefore, Terry got in a mood and wouldn't take them back so I had to organise taxi's, so even that had his control over it.

Then, a miracle happened and my son had a little girl who was born at twenty-six weeks, she was born very premature and we didn't know if she was going to make it or not and I said I wanted to go and see her in case she didn't but Terry said I wasn't allowed, so I said but what if my little girl dies and he said, 'Well that's your hard luck isn't it.'

And that made me feel sad, it made me feel cross, it made me feel like I don't want this anymore. Why should I be controlled? I have a life, I have a heart. So, at 5.00 a.m. in the morning, I escaped ... went up to Hull to see my little granddaughter, I spent two weeks up here in Hull. Just getting myself ready for a life change and I knew it was going to be a heck of a life change.

I went back to Milton Keynes, I got battered again, ended up in hospital, two weeks after that, I went to the police station at three o'clock in the morning, with the things that were important to me from my mum and dad who had passed away. I said to them that I wanted to leave, they kept me safe till the first coach, which was at something like ten o'clock in the morning. I left Milton Keynes, never to return. And I came up to Hull the long way around, I had to get off at Nottingham. But I got here.

And then started a difficult time, because after so many years of being controlled, your everyday life, you don't have. When I stayed at my sons straight after that, I couldn't even get dressed myself, that's how stupid this was. I sat there and waited for someone to say to me, 'Mum, you've got to wear this,' or 'Mum, you've got to wear that.'

And of course, that never happened. So, I started, two days after I got to Hull, I was sleeping downstairs in their living room and I looked up and there was this face at the window – it was Terry. He'd followed me.

My daughter-in-law was absolutely brilliant, she controlled the whole situation, she basically said, 'Please leave, we have children in the house, Mum doesn't want you anymore.' He made an excuse about needing a form filling out, so she said, 'post it through, we'll help you fill it out and post it back.' Then he said he had no money to get back, so she said, 'Well that's not gonna be an excuse, Terry, we'll give you some money to put in the car so that you can get back.'

So, he left.

He kept trying to get hold of me, I went on holiday. It was my first ever holiday and it was a national holiday and on the way, he kept telling me that he was going to tell the police that I was leaving the country. He was going to tell the police that I was a major drug dealer. He was going to tell social services that I was no longer in need of the money – I used to get disability because even though I wasn't in the wheelchair, I still had issues with walking and everything.

I got so scared … I nearly got off that coach because I was so frightened that the police would be waiting for me at Dover. Well, they weren't. And that was the time. That was the moment it clicked that he could no longer control me, because, hey! I'm going on holiday here!

I came back off the holiday and my life, for a little while, was fine.
I'm very loyal to promises unfortunately.

My daughter had her stroke in 2012 and because he'd always been helpful in arranging contact and everything I made one promise that if anything major happened to her, I'd always let him know. After she'd had the stroke, I let him know. So, he came down to London to visit her, he soon changed, again. He was with someone new at that point. He was there all the way through my daughter's recovery, and I thought maybe he had changed. Until one day he turned up at my daughter's and asked for a cup of tea in the old manner, I immediately recognised it. I looked at my daughter, who had her care worker with her, so she couldn't jump up and make his cup of tea – he got so aggressive – it was like, it was worse in a way because this young lady, the worker and my daughter never saw that side of him – she thought he was marvellous! And she just looked, and he got so cross and so aggressive, he even tried to go forward to grab her to drag her in the kitchen and I put myself in between her and him and he said, 'That's it, I'm leaving.' He called her a prostitute, a slut, he called me all the names under the sun and stormed out and from that day on, I never spoke to him again. I got plenty of abusive messages from him but I never spoke to him.

Life, I must admit, totally changed.

I was happier, I came back up to Hull – I lived in London for a year and half because my daughter needed to recover – we then decided, the pair of us, that we'd move up to Hull because my son was there and we were really happy. During all this, a little boy was born, but died at 25+1 and my granddaughter has a heart condition and she's under Leeds Hospital so, the family made the decision that they had to move to Leeds because the hospital was there, but my daughter and I wanted to stay here in Hull, we've made Hull our home base really.

About a year and a half ago, I went to the mercy seats and I gave my life to God and since then, I must say, my life has totally changed.

I don't feel worthless anymore. I feel like I'm a person. I've come through this so I think my message to anyone who is reading this book is, even though you might be going through a difficult time, even though you think there's no end, there is an end. It might not mean to go to God, it might not mean to go to Jesus, but there'll always be something at the end to make your life better. And I've found that with other women I've spoken to, who've been through abusive situations, that there is a point, there is a turning point, once you hit the turning point, then you move forward and then you seem to break the cycle. And the cycle is: you must have a period of time when you have no man in your life or if your abuser is of the same sex, there has to be a time when you have no one in your life because you need that time to make the changes necessary in you, that stops you being abused, you become your own person and that is so important.

There is hope.

I'd like to thank the Salvation Army Icehouse, especially Captain Layton, Captain Kinsley, and Captain Paula, for helping me beat the drugs and the smoking and bringing forward and showing me that *regardless of my past, I have worth and I am valued.*

ANNE

Int: Tell me what happened, how did it begin?

A: Okay, I met my husband in 2002, married in 2005, had our first child in 2009 and it was around that time that we started to experience our first traumas as a couple, as we'll all have them, but before then, everything was peachy. We were the life and soul of the party. When I had our eldest, he was five weeks early and I had an emergency C-section so I was out for the count for six hours and didn't recognise him as my child when I came around, everyone else had already met him before me, so that was quite hard on us. My husband was having to work to support us, I had post-natal depression, I was working in a very challenging school at the time and so I went back to school but I came off sick with stress, the school was in the process of closure so it was difficult. And then I fell pregnant with my second child and I was determined to have a natural birth, to experience it, I felt like I'd been robbed the first time and I was probably the only lady in the labour ward smiling but I enjoyed the whole experience, it was absolutely fantastic. It was almost a healer from the first birthing experience and things were great.

I took a full year off on maternity and when I went back, the school had dissolved in to such a state that it no longer represented teaching and felt more like babysitting and crowd control. And it was quite dangerous and so, I came off sick again and spent a lot of time with my daughter. She was my saviour. But unfortunately, my husband lost his job and so, after I'd been made redundant from the school when it closed down in twenty-twelve, I had to go work on supply. My nanna had been diagnosed with stage four cancer and I treated my nanna more like my mum, she was available a lot more than my mum ever was and so that was heartbreaking for me, having to nurse her through her illness for a year before she died, with a newborn and a two-year old and an unemployed husband who refused to get out of bed. And rather than asking him and talking to him, actually, that's

68

bollocks, I always make excuses for him, I did try and speak to him, lots of times and he just point blank refused to talk about it. And so, I would get mad in those days, I was almost out of control of my own emotions to the point where I would smash stuff up, I would launch stuff, I would generally be quite aggressive and that was just because I felt like a single parent and that I'd been completely abandoned as a wife. I remember speaking to my mum about it and asking if she thought I should stay with him and she said that only I could answer that. So, I thought okay, and I did.

I tried to help him lots … he's type one diabetic so whenever he suffered a bout of depression – before then it was undiagnosed so we never called it depression, he wouldn't keep on top of his insulin and his blood sugars would go haywire and that would make his behaviour quite aggressive. Whenever I mentioned to him that I felt his blood sugars were low – after nine years you got to recognise the signs – but because his brain wasn't functioning properly, he would deny it telling me to leave him alone, which would make him worse and then he'd start getting quite aggressive and I'd become concerned that this behaviour was in front of the children, the children didn't understand diabetes or how it affects you when you're not controlling it. He would slip in to fits, he'd be completely incoherent, he'd be hallucinating, he'd crying like a baby and it was really disturbing and really quite challenging for me to deal with whilst nursing my cancer riddled nanna.

Int: Did he purposely not take his insulin or was he in denial?

A: I think he was in denial. I think he felt as if it was his diabetes that had stopped him being able to achieve whatever it was he wanted to achieve in his life so he used to hate it with a passion, and when his depression kicked in, he refused to acknowledge that it existed. Saying he was fine, and thinking that if he didn't eat, he didn't have to inject. So, he, it, was all over the place. We took him to the Brocklehurst centre, which is the diabetic place and they tried to address the issue by putting him on to an insulin pump which is a thing that he wears and has an injection in it the first time, but it stays in with a little cannula so it's constantly giving him a feed of insulin. It's Bluetooth controlled so he could do it with his phone. So, if he'd had a piece of gateaux, he could put it in the app and it would adjust his insulin for a bit. But that is still dependent on whether you control the device so it was no better at all. We managed to get him a job and it was probably the best job he'd ever had in his life. I wrote his application form, I coached him for the first period because he went through a recruitment agency and initially he was a temp, and I said to him that this was his opportunity to get himself a full-time job at this very good place to work, so he was going in every day asking to be taught things, asking to be put forward for the next job, until finally he got it. So, he got the job and we were excited but because he wasn't managing his bloods and because his head wasn't in the right place and because we were trying to look after two small children and my head was slightly all over the place as well, he made the mistake of running two batches at work so he could get home quicker so he could release me from baby duty and that's what he got sacked for, so he lost that job.

Int: Was he better when he was in work?

A: Yes. He was working night shifts though, twelve-hour night shifts which was horrendous for us because he would just come in and go straight to bed and he wouldn't even spend any time with the children. But he'd be adamant that when he came in from work he had to be left alone for half an hour when he first got there because he was working and he didn't feel that he had to contribute to the running of the house or anything because I was at home and that was my job and that's what I should have been doing. That put me off because I'm not a very submissive person so ... so we used to argue a lot about that. We had a big house and I said when we bought it that I wasn't cleaning the entire house all by myself, he had to help me, but he never did and that used to eat away at me all the time. Then the more we were arguing, the more he sort of backed himself into a corner and I'd try and give him the opportunity to talk about anything and everything but he would point-blank say no. And I knew every time he did that, it was just chipping away at our marriage.

Int: How did all that make you feel?

A: I felt like my life was over. I felt like, I was thirty-two/thirty-three and I was on the scrap heap because I didn't have the chance of achieving anything I wanted to achieve, I felt like I was on the bottom of the pile when it came to everything. I knew that I had massive potential that I wasn't utilising and I think that was my biggest grievance with the whole thing – I knew I was amazing, why didn't he? Why didn't he know? He never, ever, gave me compliments for anything, even when it was so blatantly obvious that I had done something well, he would just say it was alright. He just point-blank wouldn't compliment me on anything. I think he felt a little bit as if I was threatening his manhood in some way, and I really took that to heart because I'd always communicated to him from the start that I believed in equality and if we were going to be a couple then we'd need to each bring fifty percent to the table because I'm not going to support you. I'd had boyfriends do that in the past and I wasn't into free loaders and he had to match me or …

Int: You mentioned earlier that you had spoken to your mum, she gave her own opinion that you had to make your own decision, was there anyone else that you confided in during the relationship about the things that happened?

A: There was a lady who used to live on the next street called Pamela and she was my husband's friend originally as they worked together. And when we were together, I didn't have anywhere to go whenever we had an argument and I'd leave or he would leave, actually, we would both end up going to her house – whichever of us left our home. Which put a lot of pressure on her and it is only recently that she has come out and said that she didn't feel I should have left him and that I have destroyed his life. And I thought, hang on, I've been round here and told you everything, I've been here every day since and you've never mentioned this to me before, that's two and half years' dishonesty when you were thinking that I was in the wrong the whole time. She suggested that we weren't good together, I do believe that she's had an influence over whether we get back together, because that was on the cards and I think … she's not a very nice lady … I thought she was.

Int: Could that have been his influence on her?

A: Yes, yes, plus they both have very similar personalities, they don't appreciate forward planning, they're both 'fly by the seat of your pants' people and they see anybody who's not as boring, so I used to get stick all the time for making plans or writing a list.

Int: Did you realise it was an unhealthy relationship? How did it come to an end – what happened there?

A: We were arguing a lot, we were struggling financially, it was completely one sided with the parenting, in fact I started to view him as being a negative influence on the children and when I'd been supply teaching – I'd gone back to work when he lost his job because we couldn't afford the house – so I was supply teaching after I'd just lost my nanna and that didn't work. My mental state wasn't up to dealing with year ten's last thing on a Friday, so I had to give that up and he wasn't putting any effort into finding a job and then my mum got diagnosed with cancer and she died almost a year to the day after my nanna. When my nanna died … I remember one incident clear as day and it's the one that sticks in my head, she died that morning and I'd been with her all night and it got to midnight and I passed over to my mum and my mum stayed with her until the early hours of the morning when she died and then they rang me to say that she'd died and we went up to the hospital to say my goodbyes. When we came back, I was cooking tea for everybody, he was in the front room with the kids and I just broke down, I hadn't cried up to this point and I just broke down and I was cooking tea and he came in, saw me crying and went back out and did absolutely nothing. I just felt alone at that point in time and I just collapsed in a heap on the floor and I cried and cried and I screamed and the whole street must have heard me and he just ignored me. For two hours. The kids, the kids were in there listening to him, I wonder what that taught them, to hear their mum upset and their dad preventing getting access to her and also not going to help her himself, what example of love are they getting from that?

Int: You're their example, you're their example now, hopefully, that's in the past and you'll be able to make up for that.

A: So … when my mum died, I suppose panic set in because I knew I was going to have that situation again where he just couldn't handle the grief that I was feeling and I was going to get blanked by him again. And … I didn't even give him chance.

I left.

I told him things have got so down and negative and the shit was hitting the fan. Things were hitting us more or less one after the other, we used to have a joke that we used to have that much good luck we were going to win the lottery this week or whatever ...

Int: At that point then, did you seek any help? Did you report anything to the police or someone else?

A: Oh yeah, the police used to come around quite regularly. I was making excuses for him the whole, telling them it wasn't him it was his diabetes and that is how come I ended up staying with him for two/three years but it wasn't until I realised as much as it was my responsibility to direct my sail and I knew that and I got myself out because of me, not because of him, it also made me recognise that he was responsible for directing his sail too and yes, he has created this by not managing his blood sugars and if he had have done, we'd have still been a happy family. Struggling to deal with all the shit that we had to deal with, but still, we would have been together, we would have been communicating and I fucking hate him for that because he just went on a selfish spree of *I've got diabetes and I don't like the fact I've got diabetes so fingers up to the world and fuck everybody.* That was his attitude. Me and the kids just got left behind really. But I'd always felt like a single parent so I convinced myself that leaving and being a single parent was no big deal you know, we weren't leaving, we were cutting him out so we would still exist in the situation we existed in, just without him.

Int: How are things now in your life? How is that situation, do the children still see him? Does it work?

A: I've made a conscious effort to make sure that we have an open communication between us for the sake of the kids. He moved to a flat and set up on his own and he found it difficult for a year or so because he'd never lived by himself before, he'd never managed his own diabetes with no one there to look after him and it was a learning experience for him at the age of thirty-five. And that's sort of what I wanted for him because I knew without that, either I'd be responsible for it or he'd die. And I didn't want to see either of those things happen, so I took a chance that he would not commit suicide, which he did threaten to do several times, he was sectioned at some point and he used to come round to the house quite a lot and threaten suicide and I had to get the police to come and break into his house at one time as he had sent everyone an email saying he was taking an overdose of insulin, he'd had enough, he was off, the kids would be better without him etc. etc. He wouldn't open the door and so they had to break the door down. There was another time when he did the same thing and he escaped out the back window as they tried to break the door down and then he ran off down the street and the coppers ran after him, rugby tackled him at the bottom of the street, handcuffed him, took him off for a mental health assessment, he was in the back of the ambulance hacking at his wrists with the handcuffs, he was bleeding all over the place and then sat there for an hour for someone to assess him only for them to decide there was nothing wrong with him and they let him go.

It was always because none of his aggressive behaviour ever got reported as domestic abuse. Because of the fact that he was diabetic and the fact his insulin wasn't managed, it was a medical condition not domestic abuse. I had to argue the toss when me and the kids found ourselves homeless in twenty-fifteen. He evicted all my things from the house on to the street on the first of January twenty-fifteen and we moved in with my dad for six weeks, this was just after my mum died, and I got a flat in the September, and the landlord of that place wanted to sell his house so we had to go to the council and say we're going to be homeless can we have a council house please and they said no, that the laws have changed and you can only get a council house if you're the victim of domestic abuse and when I said I had been, they disagreed. So, I got a letter from DAPP, they wrote to me before saying that they got my details from the police and thought I might need their services, I said no at the time, I said it's not his fault ... So, I had to sit with a woman at the council and argue every single police incident when they had been called out to the house and the situation that surrounded each one and why it was domestic abuse and not the medical situation and it was then that I realised in myself, all the excuses that I'd made for him, these were being recorded as medical incidents because that's the first thing that I told them when they first came in. Telling them to be careful with him because his blood sugars were low and he might do this and he might do that, I was literally on edge all the time.

I suffered a break down mid-way through 2015 and found solace in my best-friend of seventeen years, who had always had a thing for me and so he was the first person I went to after I'd split up with my husband. That didn't work and that was the final straw that broke the camel's back I think and on top of everything, I'd now lost my best mate of seventeen years. So, I just descended into not caring about anything, I used to put the kids to bed and my days used to consist of just making it through to bedtime. I never even threw any thought towards what would happen when they'd gone to bed, it was just always that that was my finish line, that was what I had to get to and then as soon as they had gone to bed I came downstairs and would literally just stare at a wall. I would sit there for two or three hours. The phone would ring, I wouldn't answer it. Needed the loo, I couldn't be arsed – I'd literally sit there until I was bursting, even though the toilet was only there – I would just shut down.

It was weird because I knew that all that was in the background but I also knew that I couldn't allow that to interfere with my ability to look after my kids because then he would have them straight away.

Int: So, it's seems like you suppressed it throughout the day …

A: Completely. I was like Jekyll and Hyde.

Int: So, going through all of that, how have you got to where you are now?

A: Honestly … Smoked a load of weed, I always have done. I smoked it for twenty-five years but when I had my breakdown it was my saviour, it was my friend, it was my confidante, it was my everything and so I spent a lot of money on it in those eighteen months. In fact, I inherited ten grand when my mum died, six grand of that I probably spent on weed. Don't tell my dad! But I'm still alive and I never bailed out on the kids, I never tried to commit suicide, I never felt out of control. And I think that was the important bit because I recognised, through my mental health training, that time is healer and that all I had to do was sit with it. And sometimes it was literally just sitting and staring at a wall, by myself. After a while of doing that you start to realise that there's cracks in your philosophy in life. I became quite promiscuous as well … I think it was probably just never having any acknowledgement from my husband over the ten years and wanting to feel like I was desirable … I wasn't interested in having relationships with any of these people. I just wanted to know that I still had it, y'know … it was great fun! Until, one day I met a guy in a bar, we exchanged numbers, me thinking that he was somebody that I already knew and he wasn't … because I was a bit drunk and so the following Saturday when I turned up at his house and he's not the guy I'm expecting … I say, 'Oh well, we'll have a date anyway, I'm here now.' And it was literally as flippant as that and he looked as me as if to say, have you got no self-respect woman? Who are you? I don't even know who you are. And any respect he'd had for me for asking for his number in a bar just fell out through the floor and I just carried on anyway. It made me cringe a little bit and that's when I started to realise I wasn't doing myself any favours and that if I were ever going to find anybody who would treat me as I deserved to be treat then I needed to start looking after myself. So, I started to appreciate the unique situation that I'd found myself in. It was only prior to that I'd felt like my life was over and I was trapped. I was in a job I hated and I'd had my kids so there was nothing to look forward to … and yet here I was, in a brand-new situation, with an absolutely blank canvass and I could go in any direction that I wanted. I am fairly intelligent and was able to construct what it was that would make me happy for the rest of my life, that's a fantastic opportunity and I've been buzzing off it ever since really. Just to be able to identify what I *like*, not what I would *prefer* to do when I'm with the kids or what me and my ex liked to do together. I was me, just me – I like second-hand shopping and I liked pampering and I liked having coffee with friends and chatting and that's how I developed my business and now I look forward to getting up for work every day.

HAYLEY WHEELER

My name is Hayley Wheeler, author of *Emotional First Aid – Life After Domestic Abuse*. My story comes from a slightly different perspective, from that of a support worker and author. In my quest to help female victims of domestic abuse, my desire to learn about the impact of abuse on women and families, I was inspired to listen, hear, and learn, I was motivated to understand and appreciate the situation, to help them find a solution. I wanted to know how it felt, how life was, what victims did differently to survivors; what perpetrators did, and the dynamics of abusive relationships as a whole.

I supported hundreds of families over nine years and found that low self-esteem was one of the commonalities in each story, it deeply resonated with me as I had low esteem for many years. Sharing such intimate details in a non-judgemental, safe environment was so important, trust was essential and empathy integral to my learning and finding the right support.

I learned that the dynamics of abusive relationships are complicated; a twisted web of deceit, fear, and a confusion of love and hate; a mass of control and manipulation. There were as many reasons for staying as there were for leaving, all valid to the victim.

To become a survivor, the victim begins to realise that they do have choices, there is another way out and they find the right support to achieve it. It became apparent that the recognition they do have a choice allows them to realise their strengths and become a survivor; the victim believes there is no way out. Mindset draws the line between staying or leaving. The women I have supported had strengths they never realised, they had skills and self-worth that had never been explored, and they had the ability to leave; my role was to support their belief and their path to a new thinking.

It came to light that the perpetrator's main role was to confuse their victim and ensure they do not have time to think, no time to talk to others, no time to be themselves. They control every second of the day, every breath they take, and every move they make. It was astounding to see how well versed the perpetrators were at playing the victim and unassumingly demanding everything from their partners. The perpetrators consumed every inch for themselves, leaving their victim with no substance, no life, no friends or family, no energy to leave. It's tiring juggling so many balls while trying to make someone who doesn't want to be happy, happy. So often, I'd hear stories of the perpetrator changing the goal posts and justifying the abuse of their partner.

Victims are led to believe that they are to blame for the abuse, that their actions, choices, or behaviour somehow cause the abuse, this is just one of the lies fed to keep a victim a victim.

The survivor recognises that the abuse is entirely the fault of the abuser, the relationship is created by two people and each person has a choice of how to behave, how to respond or react to any given situation; when the accountability replaces blame, the victim becomes the survivor.

For every woman or man feeling there is no way out from an abusive relationship – there is a way out, a way to be safe, and a way to be happy again.

You are worth it, you have value, and you deserve a life of peace and to live it your way.

BERNADETTE BARLOW

I look at my daughter now, on her tenth birthday; how happy she is, bursting with energy and loving everything about her birthday. She's bubbly, happy-go-lucky and full of fun – just as every mother should wish her daughter to be, just as I am thrilled to see that she is. Her smile says it all – how wonderful life is. Surrounded by her friends for her birthday party, my daughter is relishing the period of when she is the birthday girl, she is the centre of attention, she is the reason why all her friends are here. She does not hold her head low, her shoulders do not droop, she does not wear a mask hiding who she truly is. She is proud, her head held high, her shoulders not stooping for anyone, and her face openly showing how she feels and who she is.

I haven't told her anything yet, she's too young to hear how important her just being here is to me. I can look in wonderment at her wide-open eyes, ready to take on the world, with me at her side. I can marvel at what the last ten years have brought to me. Those words when she was born, 'she's a girl', at the time, felt like the worst words I would ever hear. The spiralling blackness, the cascading of competing emotions but the one winning out at the time being that I didn't want her, I didn't deserve her, I couldn't do right by her. I fought with all my strength to feel differently but at the time, could not. Yet my daughter never gave up on me, she looked to me to meet her needs, and patiently waited until I could. At first, these were feeding, changing, and little else and, as time passed the needs progressed to needing love, support, and encouragement to flourish. She loved me unconditionally and that spurred me through all the demons I needed to put to rest. She never expressed disappointment; she just opened her arms all the more and accepted me as I was. She looked into my eyes with such love, such confidence in me – it had to be only a matter of time before I could return the compliment. And gradually, day by day, her patience paid off – and I could love her a little more. She won my heart bit by bit – just by being her.

79

And what about me? I have learnt to love again. My daughter. My son. Myself! I am not the person I had been led to believe that I was. I am not a dirty, horrible, evil person that doesn't deserve any goodness from people in my life. I didn't deserve any of the abuse inflicted on me. That childhood was mine – it wasn't for those despicable people to steal – it didn't belong to them, it belonged to ME! I deserve to LIVE, free of those horrors forced on to me when I was a child, as my daughter is now. My eyes were not open wide – I dared not open them to anything or anyone, in fear of being abused again. I didn't laugh until my sides could take no more, I didn't giggle at silly things without any worry over the consequences, I didn't welcome anyone into my heart – it had been crushed enough. I didn't hug – imagine that! Until my daughter was born, I hadn't truly hugged anyone. I may have done the action of a hug, but I had never felt what the gift of a hug truly was. The gift of acceptance and love for the person I am hugging, and the receiving of that acceptance and love from them. I could not imagine a day passing without hugging my daughter and son now – whether physically, or by proxy if they are not with me.

The long fight, the arduous, painful, heartbreaking fight has moved me from a survivor of sexual, physical, and emotional abuse to a thriver. I have broken the cycle of abuse. I have refused the teachings I had been given as a child and young adult. I have started again; learnt how to be from scratch. I didn't know how to be a mum, how to be a woman, how to be an adult in control of my own destiny, how to love my children, how to accept love, how to give and receive, how to enjoy who I am, how to be proud to be me; it all took so much time to learn, painstakingly slow at times. But my daughter was waiting patiently for me to catch up.

I don't know whether I would advise other survivors to report those who have abused them to the police or not. It's a very personal matter, not one that can be judged by others. I feel very strongly that it must be their decision and no one else's. It must be for them, to help them move on with their lives. Why should they have the moral pressure to report when they have had so much taken from them already? They've had all their choices snatched away, their power ripped away from them. Let's empower them now, not abuse them further by insisting they should report.

We have had a lot of publicity triggered off by the discovery that Jimmy Saville had groomed and abused so many vulnerable children and adults. Other public figures have also come to light since his abuse was brought out by the media. The public has reacted in various ways, but one question that has been asked over and over is why didn't they say anything at the time?

It was over twenty years since I was abused … when I finally reported it to the police. I did try and say something at the time, I asked what I should do if a man tried to kiss me when I didn't want him to – I was sent to my room for a week. I didn't matter. Throughout my childhood I had been led to believe that I wasn't worthy of being heard, that it didn't matter that I had been abused; I was a horrible, dirty, good for nothing piece of meat. No one ever challenged that belief, no one I heard anyway. So how could I speak out? When I left my parent's house, I buried it, put it behind me, and got on with my life. Why would I want to take it with me? I convinced myself that I was okay, that now I'd left home it was no longer relevant to me.

And when I did report it to the police, now being a time when things have improved considerably in this type of case remember, I went through different periods of trauma; the system was not there to support me through the individual cases, mistakes were made, I still had to carry on fighting to get to where I wanted to be. There were postponements, crossings of t's and the dotting of i's to be made. The court cases themselves were both postponed more than once – which meant a further wait of months. In total, across the two cases, I have spent 2.5 days on the stand – most of the time being cross-examined. I learnt things of my parents that crushed me more than I thought I could ever bear. To have my parents give evidence in support of the men who had sexually abused their daughter for many years, to declare me a liar, to make out I was a whore (at age seven – fourteen?!) and behaved badly, that these men were good people – I've had to work through the heartbreak of losing it all; my parents, my ex-husband, and the family that I so yearned.

So, in hindsight – would I have still reported these two men? I most certainly would have. The whole process has grounded me, helped me work through battles that I may have otherwise shied away from. Some would not help or join me on my journey, but others did, my children did, I did. For me, the most important thing of all was that I was finally heard. The guilty verdicts meant those two men were put away and placed on the sexual offenders' register – never allowed to work with children again. Ever. So, I can now look into my daughter's eyes and truthfully say that there are no monsters.

Daughter, I love you more than words could ever say, you have shown me the world. When I look at you now, and think back to those words 'it's a girl' – they are now the best words I have ever heard.

I love the song 'Better Man' by *Thunder*. What you don't know is how the lyrics of that song are so prudent to me, to you. A day never goes by when I don't thank the stars for giving me a daughter, you, my rock, my daughter.

ELYSE BUELL

When I was twenty, I met this guy who I thought was everything. We moved in together within weeks, we were engaged within nine months, and got married two years after we met. I thought we had a perfect marriage, with only a few speed bumps.

It took me walking away from the situation to realise just how toxic the relationship was.

The signs were all there, right from the beginning. The first time I met his parents, his mother looked me right in the face and asked him why he had to date someone that was fat. There was always some kind of abusive comment in my direction, and while it started with his family, it eventually spread to him. Even his siblings, who were younger by ten to fifteen years, were verbally abusive. They often accused me of being a gold digger, even though we both had good jobs. I was often not allowed in the house when I made his mother mad, and would have to sit in the car and wait for him.

I was never allowed to go anywhere alone: the grocery store, a friend's house, or even to see my parents. At first, I thought it was cute, that he always wanted to be with me. I didn't realise until much later how controlling it was. He wouldn't let me go back to school to finish my degree because it was a 'waste of money'. He had a good job, and could support us, and it made no sense to him.

He never hit me physically but he hit me emotionally and mentally. If he did get physical, it was always at the expense of the bathroom door or a window. I never had any privacy. I would try to lock myself in the bathroom to have some peace and quiet, and he would kick the door down, breaking the chain lock. I replaced that lock more than a dozen times. There was one time when we got into an argument at his parents' house, and for some reason, his parents were siding with me. I was sitting on the porch with his parents, and he picked up a huge rock, about a foot long, and threw it in our general direction.

It missed us, but did some serious damage to the side of his parents' house. We had to foot the $2,000 bill to have the siding replaced. He would punch windows in our apartment and shatter them. At the time, our road was under construction so we always blamed flying debris, and our landlord would have it replaced. I always figured that if he kept his hands off me, everything was okay.

We had some financial issues when we first lived together as we were young and irresponsible. It took a toll on his credit, so as we started making more money and fixing mistakes, we started taking out credit cards, all under my name. At the height of it, we had nine credit cards, several of which were store credit cards that had impossibly high interest rates. After totalling a second car, while we were still making payments on the first car, we had to take out the loan for the new car under my name. When we split, he took the car because I couldn't afford the payments, but I was stuck with all the credit cards. I didn't even make half of what he made, and I couldn't even afford the monthly payments on all of them. It took me almost three years to pay off all the cards.

I thought that a geographic change would be good. We lived in a rough area and had witnessed some violence and break-ins. We moved a town over, to a bigger apartment in a nicer neighbourhood. For some reason, I thought it would fix us. It wasn't until I couldn't make excuses for the broken windows anymore that I realised that I couldn't do it any longer. I started having panic attacks every time I was home. I would lock myself in the bathroom or closet just to have the door kicked down and get yelled at for 'being a crazy person.' Eventually, he took all the door knobs off our doors so I couldn't lock myself in anywhere. I had no place for any privacy.

I started drinking heavily to calm the panic attacks. I would start drinking as soon as I got home so I could be blacked out in bed by the time he came home. I had friends who would come to my house and clean up the empty cans and bottles so that he wouldn't see how much I was drinking. One glass of wine turned into a bottle, and bottles turned into boxes, wine turned into whiskey. The worse our relationship got, the worse my drinking got. We eventually decided to separate, but because we had a lease on this apartment that we couldn't get out of, we had to stay. He also didn't want to admit to

84

his parents that we were separating, so I was still required to go to family dinners and functions every week. I had to drink the whole way there, and drink the whole way back just to deal with it. I stayed in one room, he stayed in the other. There were fights every day and they progressively got worse. I left for vacation and when I came back, he had moved out. He bounced the rent check and I couldn't afford it on my own so I got evicted. I was fortunate enough to have family that had a place for me to live.

My family thought it was endearing that he always went grocery shopping with me and would come to visit with me. I never told them about the fights or the damage that had been done. The night before our wedding, my mom asked us if this was what we really wanted. Did I really want to be attached to his family for the rest of my life? My naïve answer was yes, because love conquers all. Years later, when I finally broke down and told my mom what was happening, she told me that I was just overreacting, that I was just complaining because I wasn't getting my way. She came over for dinner one night, and he was grilling on the patio. She was sitting outside with him, and he yelled in to ask me to bring him something. I accidentally brought the wrong thing out, and he proceeded to throw it back at me, while cursing and screaming. My mom was in shock, she'd never seen this side of him. It was hard for my family to see the side I saw, and even years later, my little sister sided with him. They never fully knew what I went through.

My divorce took three years to finalise, and he still tried to sink his hooks in. He took over six months to sign the separation paperwork and we had to wait a year after that to file for divorce. When I attempted to file, I found out that he hired a lawyer to rewrite our separation paperwork. A six-page document became a twenty-five-page document. He wanted me to notify him of every phone number, address, and job change that I had for the rest of my life. He wanted to know where I was, even though we weren't together anymore. It took another year to finalise this paperwork to where I was satisfied, and another six months after that to finalise the divorce. After receiving my divorce papers, his lawyer had it written in there that I was allowed to return to my previous name, but failed to note what my name used to be. Most places won't accept the paperwork, and I still have several things with his name on it. I can't do anything about it until I can afford to do a legal name change and get it court approved.

When it finally ended, and I looked back, I realised the damage that had been done. The damage that still haunts me today. I still have trust issues and it doesn't take much to spike my anxiety. I got sober about a year and a half after the separation. I'm coming up on three years sober now. I went back to school, and I'm halfway through my bachelors in psychology, with a concentration in addiction counselling. I took up a hobby doing nail art and it's since evolved into a business, one that has given me freedom. I was able to pay off my debt and I'm driving a brand-new car. I've regained my confidence and gained a sense of freedom … something I haven't had in a long time.

The most important thing is that I learned to love myself, to be happy, and to be independent.

EMMA ROSCOE

'Sticks and stones may break my bones but words will never hurt me'.

If that was true I wouldn't have a story to share with you and I certainly wouldn't be the woman I am today, but my strength and resilience didn't come easily. I've been in some dark places mentally and emotionally and had to claw my way back more than once. All because of the hurt and long-term damage caused by the words and behaviours of a man who 'loved' me, the blame I carried and self-loathing I felt, as a result.

I was twenty-six when I handed him back the engagement ring I'd been wearing for the past seven years and ended our relationship. He'd been my first 'love', the one I'd lost my virginity to and the one I thought I'd spend the rest of my life with. But he was also the one who had broken me, had worn me down and turned me into a woman I neither recognised nor wanted to be anymore. I felt like I was dying inside and had reached a point of no return. It was two weeks after our 10th anniversary together that my 'realisation switch' had been flicked on. He'd been and picked up details of local properties for sale and started talking about deposits and mortgages and what we might be able to afford, but it was all just noise in my head and I could feel the panic rising through my body. I couldn't do this anymore, I didn't want to marry him, I didn't want him to be the father to my future children and I sure as hell didn't want to buy a bloody house with him! I had a million panicked thoughts running through my head and I felt like I couldn't breathe. I had no words. But as it turned out I didn't need any because he knew. My face and the vacant look my eyes where he'd no doubt hoped to see excitement, were telling him for me. His whole world had just come crashing down around him. I didn't want this anymore and he could tell. In that moment, everything had changed. I felt both scared and empowered at the same time. He broke down and kept saying, 'Please don't say it, don't say it's over,' and so ... I didn't.

I didn't say it.

I said nothing at all.

As we lay in bed he cried himself to sleep and I just lay there thinking, *fuck! What do I do now?!*

In the morning, he pleaded with me to take some time, to think things over and not make a decision yet. I said, 'okay', but in my head, I knew it wouldn't change anything. Emotionally, I think I'd finally left him some months before. As scary as this situation was, in many ways it was just a practicality now. I wasn't going to change my mind; no amount of time would change my decision and I silently made a promise to myself not to back down. Not this time. Not ever again.

Tearful telephone calls, pleading, saying he couldn't live without me and endless promises to change ensued over the next five days before I returned to see him. When I arrived, he asked me if he could have a hug and held out his arms. I just looked at him, again no words but he knew. I took a deep breath and looked him in the eyes as I told him that each time he'd hurt me, falsely accused me of something, scared me, or made me cry, I'd loved him a little bit less than before and that now there was nothing left.

No love ... nothing.

I still don't know where I found the courage to do it, I just knew I had to. I think I must have been running on adrenaline from knowing that I had reached the point of no return. I had two choices ... leave now or succumb to a life of surviving in the moment, treading on eggshells, and merely existing.

As I got in my car to go, I was shaking, fumbling with the gear stick and trying to steady my foot on the clutch, I felt like I was going to throw up and could feel the panic rising up my body again. I'd done it ... I'd finally done it. I didn't look back as I drove away. I was breaking free. I'd taken back control.

The talk of houses and mortgages had been the straw that broke the camel's back so to say, but there had been a gradual burn up to that point. My strength hadn't instantaneously kicked in that night. I'd been working myself up to it for several months, getting mentally stronger and daring to almost believe that there could be something better than this for me out there but at the same time, having no idea how to break away. For years he'd had all the control, I'd back down every time and apologise because he always managed to get me to the point where I took responsibility for what had happened and what he had done. It was always my fault that he'd got angry, or upset or paranoid ... again. My fault that he'd lost control or got to that level of drunkenness or been completely stoned. My fault that he'd got jealous and got in a fight or smashed his car up. My fault he'd made me cry or kicked in the door or punched the wall ... again.

I would always end up in tears, he'd always manage to find it in his heart to 'forgive me', nine times out of ten, we'd 'make up' by having sex that I didn't really want but just resided to have. Saying no or resisting his efforts at showing me how much he loved me, only ever ended in further suspicion that I must be getting it elsewhere or further false accusations, so it was easier and safer for me to just go along with it and hate myself that little bit more each time for being so weak.

You see, those words had done some damage over the years.

The put-downs, the blaming, the accusations, the passive aggressive behaviours always did more harm to me than him losing his temper and smashing things up. Don't get me wrong, I was scared many times, but it was his words that had destroyed parts of me inside. The fear just added to it, keeping me in my place and creating an invisible line that I never dared to cross. At least not until those last few weeks. For several years after it was over, I was ashamed to admit to this, but the sad truth is that I'd steadily reached the point where I actually wanted him to hurt me. It's sickening in many ways but in my desperation to not be with him anymore, I wanted him to do something so bad that I'd have no excuse not to leave him. I thought that if he physically hurt me, there would be something visible that I couldn't hide from other people. They'd see he'd done something awful to me and they'd understand why I didn't want to be with him. Nobody would judge or blame me. It wouldn't be my fault. It would be over because of him and people who knew us both would understand why.

That's the depths of what I'd been driven to, it was as though I needed permission and the approval of others to leave him. In writing this now I feel, in part, that shame again, but then I think about how far I've come and remind myself of the life I have now and then all that shame disintegrates because it doesn't have a hold on me anymore.

During the time we were together, I became very good at hiding what was going on and what things were really like from all my friends and family. I even started to believe the bullshit stories and excuses myself. Some people have since told me that they thought we had the perfect relationship. I guess I must have been pretty convincing in the facade I had created. It was almost as though by painting that picture and never discussing what really went on, I was kidding myself that things were okay. That this was 'normal'. That this was what relationships were like. That this was what love was like. But deep down, I knew that love wasn't about hurting and accusing and blaming. That being in love with someone didn't give them the right to check your phone, to tell you what you could and couldn't wear, what you could and couldn't do and where they did and didn't want you working or going out. I knew that being in love wasn't about isolating me from my friends, letting me down constantly by not turning up to family meals out they'd promised to attend, or continuously borrowing money off me to consequently never give it back.

The sixteen-year-old Emma who fell into the wrong kind of love with the wrong boy learnt a lot of things about herself over those ten years, but lost a lot of herself too.

The emotional abuse and control I experienced affected me for many years after I left. My thought patterns, my behaviour, the way I saw others and crucially, the way I saw myself. It affected my self-confidence, my self-belief and I would blame myself and think I was a failure if things went wrong. Depression and anxiety have reared their unwelcome heads a few times, which would often bring with them panic attacks. I had counselling and CBT and, I began to admit to myself, and others, some of what had gone on between me and him over the years.

In my early thirties, I had four miscarriages which a consultant couldn't find any medical reason for and I found myself again questioning whether it was my fault. Through further counselling I was able to finally 'forgive' myself and end the self-punishment for staying in that situation for all those years. I wasn't to blame for his

90

behaviour and words. I always had deserved better and I now truly believed that I deserved to be happy and to be a mum.

Learning to accept and love myself again was a long and difficult journey but now that ten-year chapter of my life no longer defines me.

I am Emma.

I am a survivor and this is my story.

HANNAH

Looking back, I should have seen it happening; I curse myself for being so blind.

I met him on a night out, a friend of a friend. I never thought he'd look twice at me but he did. We got together and two weeks later he proposed and we began looking for a house together.

He'd arrange nights out for us with his friends, he said he wanted to show me off. It was nice feeling wanted but when we'd get there he'd just spend time with his friends. To be honest, at first, it was a pleasant change after being in a relationship where the partner was entirely dependent on me. With hindsight, I can see that these nights always coincided with times I would've normally been out with my friends – but that's normal in a new relationship, right? Or at least that's what I told myself at the time. Slowly, my friendship circle dwindled away to nothing, and all I had were the girlfriends of his friends.

Anyway, a few months passed, we found a house and he made me believe that because I was between jobs, I shouldn't be on the mortgage – I agreed, he was the financially stable one. I felt guilty though, so he told me that I could contribute to the work he wanted to do to the house. I took out a £10,000 loan whilst I was waiting to hear back about a job. When we moved in he told me I had to pay the utility bills because I was in the house more than him – even though I was also working full-time then too. I agreed, because what else could I do? I'd just found out I was pregnant and he'd made himself my whole world, and he'd certainly made it clear no one else would want a pregnant girl with ongoing health issues. Unfortunately, I had a miscarriage and he told me to 'flush it away' and later told his family that medics had said it was because I'd taken my medication … he hadn't even let me see a doctor afterwards, but they were all blaming me.

After the miscarriage, my body took a while to recover, so he made me do certain sexual acts; ones I initially protested about but was pressured into as he told me it was 'what couples do'. He was my first sexual partner, excluding a violent rape, so I knew no different and went along with it. Combine that with his ongoing jibes about my looks, post-pregnancy body, and my health, and he truly managed to convince me that without him I'd be alone forever.

A few years passed and it all just continued in the same vein, until I experienced a major trauma. It was then that some of my friends started to rally round. One night, after I'd spent the whole day babysitting his younger cousin, those friends took me to the cinema to try and distract me. Halfway through the film, I got a text telling me not to go home that night. I was distraught. He wouldn't tell me why, only that I could go and collect some clothes for the next day. When I saw him the next day he told me that I'd made his life a misery for four years and he couldn't take it anymore and he'd be changing the locks. I was homeless.

Thankfully, my friends took me in, and that was when it all began to unravel ... all the lies he'd told me, how much of my life he'd controlled ... how my friends had tried to tell me but he'd intercepted their messages and replied as me, telling them to leave me alone. It was then that I realised that the reason he wouldn't have internet installed in the house was so he could stop me having any social media accounts for several years – limiting my means of contacting friends.

Fast forward and I'm now seven years free of that relationship, however, I still feel the impact. Whilst some of my friends are now back in my life, there are a lot who feel that it was my choice to burn those bridges; I wish they could see the guilt I still carry. My current partner is amazing and couldn't be any more different, but I still worry he'll leave me and I'm scared to give up any of my independence for fear of being left with nothing again. I still get upset if I misconstrue a comment he makes or if he tries to joke about something that reminds me of the time.

I'm healing and I know my life is better now.

HELEN PRYKE

When I was fifteen, I found out that the man I thought was my father was in fact my stepfather. When I was seventeen, my mum died from breast cancer. When I was eighteen, I left home and moved in with a man I'd only known for three months.

Looking back, my childhood was the catalyst to everything else that happened in my adult life. I was a quiet, shy child who learnt from an early age to be aware of the people around me, their expressions and their moods, in order to avoid being shouted at or picked on. The man I thought was my dad treated me differently from my brother and sister, and I thought that was my fault, that there was something wrong with me. Mum was the one stable thing in my life, the only person I could depend on, and when she died it left a hole that no one could ever fill.

When I met an Italian man, it seemed the perfect way to leave my old life and start a brand-new future, full of possibilities. I was eighteen, he was thirty-three. Little did I know that it would be a case of out of the frying pan and into the fire. I was too young to cope with his incessant flirting with other women, his frequent trips abroad for work, the silent treatment when I did something wrong. I realised I'd made the biggest mistake of my life just a few months after moving in with him, but by then it was too late. I'd burnt my bridges with my stepfather, brother, and sister the day I walked out without saying anything. My nan and uncle were supportive, but thought he was a wonderful person – how could I tell them otherwise. I worked, had friends, had my own life outside of the relationship, so carried on through the good times and bad.

Then he dropped the bombshell. His company had ordered him to go back to Italy. I had two choices: stay in the UK, living in a bedsit, or move to Italy with him. I was almost twenty, I'd never lived alone before, I was slowly being cut off from my friends and family. It was a no-brainer – I moved to Italy.

I had to learn a new language, a new culture, a completely different way of living, and try to integrate into a family that didn't seem to like me or want me there. Stuck in a small apartment in Milan all day, with no job and no friends, I went from having all the freedom I needed, to feeling like a caged animal. Moving to a semi-detached house in the countryside helped a bit – I had more space, and made a couple of new friends.

It wasn't until my oldest son was six and started school that I realised just how abnormal my marriage was. I met other parents; we started going out to restaurants and socialising with them, and I saw how much they loved and respected each other. Unlike me, they could make jokes about their partners without fear of retribution, and their public displays of affection were genuine demonstrations of their love. I admit that I felt jealous of them, of their freedom to behave as they wanted in front of their husbands and friends, of that obvious intimacy that they had as a couple and a family.

I mentioned retribution – but it was never physical, never violent. If it had been, I would have got out of the relationship a lot sooner. I'd always said I would never let a man hit me. But psychological abuse is very different, most of the time you don't realise it's even happening. The abuser gradually wears you down until you believe what they're saying, you start blaming yourself for everything, and you no longer have your own personality. That's what happened to me. I wore clothes that were suitable for a woman in her sixties, chosen together with my husband. I went grey at an early age, thanks to genes inherited from Mum's side of the family, but never dyed my hair as he convinced me that it would be too expensive and time consuming. I stayed at home looking after the kids while he travelled the world for his work. I never went out alone and if I wanted to see a friend, I'd have to tell him exactly where and when. When I got my driving licence, at the grand old age of thirty-one, I thought things would change. We had two cars, so I could use one of them. Boy, was I wrong. I had to ask to use the car and tell him where I was going and why. If I bought clothes for the kids I had to produce receipts, so that he could 'keep an eye on our finances'.

Things came to a head after twenty-three years, in 2009. He started becoming more verbally aggressive, more critical of the children, and even violent at times. When I saw that my children were suffering, I found the courage to make an appointment with a lawyer. It was the first time I'd spoken with someone about what I was going through. She listened to me, and then told me that I was being psychologically, emotionally, and economically abused. I'd had no idea, but as we talked everything fell into place.

The months before the separation became legal were hell – he was still in the house, and becoming more and more aggressive. He would hold my shoulders and shout at the top of his voice in my ear, blaming me for everything; even now, I flinch at loud noises and don't like being touched by anyone. I tried to protect my two children as much as I could, but they saw what was happening and were deeply affected by it, and still have problems today.

Then, a couple of months after he'd finally left the house and we were getting our lives back on track, there was another bombshell. We found out that he had a brain tumour. I was blamed by his family, his work colleagues, his friends, even by the doctors for not having realised what was going on. And I was under incredible pressure to take him back, from everyone. Except one friend, who told me, in no uncertain terms, that he would make my life hell if I went back to him. I knew she was right. So, I carried on with the divorce proceedings, fighting against everyone, knowing that I was doing the right thing for myself and my children.

Seven years later, I am remarried to a man who is the complete opposite. We make fun of each other, we hug and kiss all the time, we hold hands wherever we go, and we are both free to be ourselves. We have our bad times too, like everyone, but we talk and explain our points of view, and we listen to each other.

My ex is still trying to make my life hell, threatening to take me to court, not paying for his kids, and writing aggressive emails. I refuse to talk to him on the phone or in person, my only contact is via email or messages, and that is kept to the minimum. I go regularly to my lawyer, as he's always threatening me with something; she has almost become a friend over the years. Yes, I am stronger now, and more able to deal with things, but some days it all gets too much still and I'm reduced to tears and desperation. Finding the strength to carry on is hard sometimes, especially as I have an auto-immune disease and my energy levels are low at the best of times. But I have a great support network of friends and family, and my husband is always there for me, fighting right alongside me. I know I will get through this.

MICHAEL

I had been single for many years, never having had a serious relationship, I had been married to my work as the saying goes, having been ambitious and hungry for constantly improving myself and having a desire to be constantly learning. As a result, I often changed jobs, moved around the UK, and always had more than one job at a time.

In 2008, I made the dreadful decision of putting too many eggs into one basket and found myself without much work because of a company that I signed a major contract with going into administration. I spent a few years caring for my elderly grandfather who had dementia and did some part-time work.

In 2011, I entered into a relationship with a beautiful young lady (fifteen years younger than myself), I was so happy, even though I was so much older, this seemed perfect. I realised at the beginning that there would be cultural issues to resolve, I was in my mid-thirty's, she was nineteen. She liked going out into town with her friends, I'd rather stay at home and listen to the radio.

We had so much in common and I was always willing to pick her up after a night out, but it became clear that she had the same traits as her narcissistic, alcoholic mother, although my partner was not an alcoholic, when she had been drinking, she became violent and frankly nasty.

Really early on, I ended up with a police verbal warning as she accused me of domestic violence, despite the fact I did nothing, it was her that smashed a hole in the door at my grandad's house and smashed ornaments and photos from his mantelpiece. This was after one of her nights out drinking.

The relationship lasted for over six years until I ended it, I could not take any more of the abuse that had become daily, persistent, and dragged me down to be half of the person that I had been previously.

In 2012, about eighteen months into our relationship, we moved in together, everything seemed perfect at the start, but things soon started going downhill, it didn't help that she had family bereavement after bereavement over the first two years of living together and she went into a deep depression, she stopped seeing her friends and her alcoholic mother and father both fell out with her, her mother sent her constant, daily abuse by text message.

I was the only constant, supporting figure in her life and I put the way she treated me down to her depression, but now I realise it was not the depression, but her character. I vowed never to desert her but after six years I could take no more of her emotional abuse.

I was repeatedly put down, made to feel stupid, she hated my family, and would always be 'ill' when there was a family gathering, I would only see my mum about four times a year, even though she only lived thirty minutes' drive away.

I wasn't allowed to see my family, I have never visited my grandad in his care home, even though I lived with him as his carer for three and a half years before he moved into it.

It got to the point where I wasn't even allowed to work, I was expected to lay in bed all day with her, while she spent all day on her phone, on Facebook chatting to other men, if I dared to chat to other women she would message them making up stories about me. I have so many people that were friends who now don't talk to me.

I had a temporary job at a university, she made sure that didn't last as she emailed the HR department telling them that I was a paedophile and made up some horrendous allegations about me, as a result, I was summarily dismissed without an investigation, as I was only a casual employee, they felt that they could take her word over mine.

This year, in 2017, she read an article on emotional abuse and read out the signs and symptoms, then told me that she had been abused all of her life by her parents, family, and her ex-partner – he was a nasty piece of work and really did physically and emotionally abuse her, but she could not see that her constant name calling and put downs directed at me was, in fact, emotional abuse – in her eyes it was banter.

The abuse included:

Name calling

Public humiliation

Preventing me from seeing family or friends

Preventing me from working

Destroying my self-confidence

Constantly accusing me of cheating, lying, and being deceitful

Constantly putting me down and telling me that I'm stupid and that my mum didn't bring me up properly as I'm an idiot

Telling me that she couldn't be with me, dumping me, and then telling me she didn't mean it – she dumped me six times in 2017 before I ended the relationship

I have a number of long-term health conditions which includes a hearing impairment – as I cannot hear conversation from one room to the next – I was constantly ignoring her – at least that is what she would claim and she would get really angry when I was lying in bed next to her and couldn't hear what she was saying – I wasn't allowed a hearing aid and my health conditions were always embarrassing to her!

She never did any housework or cooking, it was my job, which was fine, but as I have several long-term health conditions this caused problems as we would have pots building up and bins that needed emptying, even when I was so ill I was in agony, I was expected to do everything, I cannot recall a time when she even made me a drink.

Finances were a big issue, as we were not earning much, I worked but hardly ever, we had very little money coming in, yet it was okay to buy lots of clothes and I'm talking about several thousand pounds worth of clothes each year, leaving me with massive debts, currently around £30,000. The only thing I insisted on was that we had to pay our bills so that we had a roof over our head and electricity and water.

She would throw massive tantrums and not talk to me for days at a time, other than to tell me I was a sh*t boyfriend. About three years into our relationship, I was considering engagement and she point-blank told me that she would never marry me. I thought maybe she's not ready to get married, maybe she wants to be better first. I was clearly just naive.

I felt as though I was constantly being put down, made to feel worthless, and treated like dirt on her shoe.

My self-confidence has been shot to pieces and I am only just starting to rebuild my life. Even now, while I write this account I'm getting messages that say, 'you never know what you had until to let it go', 'you'll miss me', and 'you'll never find anyone as good as me'. Plus, many more messages that are so much worse.

I really wish I had left three years ago when the relationship changed, but at the time I was not able to see straight, I thought things would work out.

I haven't been able to confide in anyone, not even about being sexually abused as a teenager, I will not go into that here, but that has been a secret that I've kept for more than twenty-five years, one day I will be ready to discuss that. In terms of the domestic abuse, I could see what was happening to me, but I couldn't get out until this year.

I'm so pleased that I did end the relationship in June 2017 and I'm so pleased that I am starting to rebuild my life and I am working. My health is improving through treatment that I wasn't allowed to seek before and I am looking for a new home, so that I can leave the shared home – currently I live in fear that she will just turn up at any time. I can't wait to end this tenancy and move on altogether.

The situation now is that we do not talk, I get abusive text messages – sounds just like her mother's behaviour. She turns up at the flat every now and then, which usually leads to arguments.

I am working, although as not as much as I would like, my health conditions are being managed more effectively and I'm in the process of finding somewhere to live. I have never bad-mouthed her to the family members that are still interested. This is the most negative account of the relationship, and by keeping my last name out of the account it provides me with a bit of anonymity.

The best bit is that I actually feel like I have a bit of a life, in one week I went out for a meal with a friend, had a long conversation on the phone with an old friend from many years ago, and talked late into the night with my cousin, things that I would never have been allowed to do just three months ago, and I see my mum at least once a week.

It's too early to say what the future holds, but right now I am working on improving my career, I've started a degree and I am currently looking at properties and hope to be moved within the next couple of months.

LAUREN STARK

I was only ten years old when it first happened; when the man I loved, trusted, and called Grandad, first touched me intimately. At first, I didn't know what it meant. I assumed it was part of the whole grandad – granddaughter relationship. It went on for a never-ending two years. He did it around my little sister, who was four years younger than me. She never saw anything. He always called it 'our secret', which I thought made us stronger than ever. He was not my biological grandad, but my step-grandad. He treat me like his own and I loved him for that.

I soon started secondary school. The curriculum included RE (religious education). For some reason, the class was on the subject of sexual assault. And it clicked. What Grandad was doing was not right, he was taking advantage of a naive eleven-year-old who did not know right from wrong. Did this mean he was doing it to my little sister? Grandad was a tall, big-boned man. If I told him to stop, what would he do? Would he be angry? What if he started doing it to my little sister? Unaware of what to do and who to turn to, I let this arrangement go on for another year. Within that year, Grandad realised I knew it was wrong and started to bribe me. I remember being told if I let him have sex with me he'd buy me the latest mobile phone.

My relationship with my mum was disastrous. We couldn't be in a room more than five minutes without screaming at each other and wanting to rip each other's heads off. I was blaming her. How dare she let her stepfather do this to me? How dare she let me go every Sunday when she knew what was happening? Deep down I knew she didn't know it was happening, I knew it wasn't her fault. I also became awful at school. Not a class went by without having an argument with a teacher or another classmate.

During one RE class, the sexual assault/rape subject crept back up.

Some student found it a laughing matter and thought it was hilarious to shout, 'my grandad is a rapist'. Something clicked in my head. I needed to tell someone. I walked out of the classroom in floods of tears. I went into the school canteen and waited for the deputy head to find me and punish me for walking out of class. Instead it was the pastoral assistant, Mrs Hill. I will never forget that woman. She was my guardian angel in my time of need. Through all my tears I managed to tell her everything. She sat and listened whilst I poured my heart out. She held my hand all day, told me everything was going to be okay. She told me she had to inform the police and social services. I instantly felt a weight being lifted off my shoulders. It was all over. The beginning of the end. Before I knew it, a social worker was sat in front of me alongside a police officer. Mrs Hill had told them most of the story so I didn't have to repeat myself. And then the dreaded time had come. The social worker told me that I had to tell my parents. Grandad was a lollipop man at a crossing close to home. So, the police officer and social worker agreed to take me home. It was the first time I had been in the back of a police car and had not been in trouble. By the time we got home, my mum was stood at the door waiting for an explanation on why I had been brought home in a police car. My dad was still at work. There was only my mum and my sister in. When my sister had gone upstairs, we all sat in the living room. I was sat next to the social worker. She turned to me and said, 'I think it would be better coming from you'. I turned to my mum and it rolled off the end of my tongue. 'Grandad Pete has been sexually abusing me.' She broke down. She was hysterical. It hit me. My mum loved me. She cared for me. The social worker sent me upstairs whilst she spoke to my mum. Not long after, my dad came home from work. I heard him walk into the living room asking what I had done now. And then silence. I heard nothing for twenty minutes. The police officers and social worker left. My dad came running upstairs and give me the biggest bear hug. He told me he was angry he couldn't protect me.

Over the following days I had to have a video interview. It felt like I was only in there half an hour, when it turned out I was in there for four and a half hours.

I didn't understand much but I was told he would be taken to court. A few months after I found out he had pleaded guilty, received two years in prison but got out after sixteen months on good behaviour.

I got my head down at school, passed all my GCSEs, went on to do my A Levels and started to study at university. Life at home got a lot easier as well. My mum and I stopped arguing and we started talking and slowly but surely became friends rather than mother and daughter.

When I was twenty, I fell pregnant and had a beautiful little boy. And then it dawned on me. What if I couldn't protect him like my parents couldn't protect me? I suffered with severe post-natal depression (and still do) and had countless therapy sessions. I work very hard to battle my demons on a daily basis. But I have a good support network to keep me going.

TANYA

Basically, I'd been diagnosed with cancer. I lost all my hair while having chemotherapy. One time in particular he told me how ugly I was (I'm not the prettiest of women with hair, so without hair I really was ugly). How 'Off putting' I was when he was trying to eat his tea with me in the room. And then, after I had been at the hospital for eight hours having treatment, I returned home tired and he just laughed and said, 'Fuck, you're ugly,' he then followed me upstairs, shouted at me, and threatened to stab me, to put me out of my misery!

I was in floods of tears ... because I cried, he pushed me so hard I almost fell over the landing banister. I was so weak after chemo but luckily, I found strength to stop myself from going over the top of the banister and going head first down the stairs.

I rang his mum who came around. He just sat laughing, no apologies. He wasn't from a rough family or anything.

He also punched me, again just after chemotherapy, when I was at my weakest. I had a bruise at the top of my left arm. The following day my MacMillan nurse visited me, she saw it. If it hadn't been for her seeing it I doubt I would have said anything as I was so scared. I opened up and told her everything. I ended up doing a moonlight flit while he was out fishing.

At the time, I did ring the police once but they mentioned about putting me through to another department and I couldn't wait as he was due home at any minute, so I put the phone down without reporting him.

Now, though, I am cancer free. In a very happy loving relationship with my soulmate.

WANDA STERNBERG

I grew up on five acres in a rural area near Seattle along with my twin sister, older sister, and younger brother. My parents worked hard to provide for us and they provided a loving atmosphere; I'd say we were a pretty normal, middle-class family.

My twin was the more outgoing, vocal type; I was always the quiet, contemplative one. In school, I never wanted to be the center of attention, I felt more comfortable not being noticed too much. I wanted to be like everyone else, but I never quite felt like I belonged. I wore glasses, braces on my teeth, and had acne. I perspired easily and often had the telltale wet armpits to prove it. I was one of the kids that nobody really wanted to be next to. I did have my circle of friends, who mostly shared the same physical appearances that I had. We all got along nicely. Not being one of the more popular crowd in school, I was not asked out by boys so I did not have any real experience in that type of relationship throughout my grammar school years.

I was a follower type and a bit of a perfectionist. I did not like to make decisions; I did not want to be wrong. Consequently, decisions were often made for me and I went along. Sometimes, this was not in my best interest. I dabbled in drugs and alcohol. I went off to college because it was what I thought was expected of me. I soon became involved with a boy and we spent the semester partying, drinking, and doing drugs. I failed school and came home. I continued to follow the path of least resistance which was to do what I thought everyone else wanted, thinking that was the path to happiness.

I enjoyed partying with my friends. Drinking gave me courage to be more outgoing. I had other boyfriends and a lot of one-night stands. Nothing in the relationships seemed to fulfil what I thought I wanted. I wanted the fairy tale; the knight in shining armor who would whisk me off my feet and take care of me for the rest of my days, living happily ever after. What I got was another story.

My first husband was a good looking, soft-spoken man. We met at a tavern where we both liked to drink beer and play pool along with our mutual friends. We moved in together and decided to get married. I became pregnant a month before our wedding. We both held jobs, although he wasn't entirely happy with his. I made the mistake of suggesting he could look for a different job. He quit work and decided that we should live off the land, growing our own food, and living off the grid. I was pregnant with our second child at that time and we moved into a small, A-frame cabin on property owned by his parents. We did have electricity, a wood burning cook stove, and an outhouse for a bathroom. We had a phone installed after much persuading on my part (in case of emergencies). He did not want me to work, although I did work as a maid at a local motel. We raised rabbits for meat, chickens for eggs and meat, and we had goats for milk. He planted a garden and would spend hours watching the plants grow. We tried raising geese as well. When there were any problems with the animals, his solution was to shoot them and use them for their meat. Animals were not for pets; their purpose was only to provide. He wanted to stay isolated from people as much as possible. It was difficult for me to talk to family or friends as he would want to know every detail of every conversation. He was never physically abusive but looking back, I can see how he tried to always be in control and keep me isolated. I was unhappy this way. I wanted more out of our life together. I wanted more for our children. I did not know how to express myself well and my only thought was of escaping the lifestyle and trying to find something better for myself and our children. I left and moved to another state to be closer to my own family where I felt supported. We divorced and I proceeded to raise the girls on my own, with the support of my family.

I felt ashamed for divorcing. I was raised at a time when divorce was on the rise, but still considered shameful. My dad was a beer drinker and I had acquired a taste for it. It was during this time I started to drink more and more as a means of escaping my feelings of shame. I worked full-time and would come home, drink a beer or two or three while preparing dinner for my children. I would then continue to drink until I was ready for bed. This became my way of coping.

I was renting my own place and was doing my best to provide for my children but I was lonely, full of shame, and mostly unhappy with my situation. My second husband came to me by way of my dad. He did work for my dad and was asked to the house I was renting to clean the pine needles off the roof. Sometime later, he showed up at my door with a case of beer and a smile. We hit it off and so began a relationship that would turn in to my nightmare. Another good-looking man but not like my previous husband. He was tall which made him somewhat intimidating. It didn't take long to become sexually active and I eventually fell pregnant. He'd had some troubles in town, getting into a fight and he got a DUII. He'd left town for some reason I don't recall and I found out I was pregnant while he was away. He'd shown me some of his tough side, talking himself up quite a bit, I think to show others just how tough he was. He was not an educated man although he had graduated high school. He was a laborer and had a good work ethic. I think part of my attraction to him was that he had stood in front of me one evening with tears in his eyes saying he just wanted to be part of a family like mine. He'd grown up the eldest of eight children and had a controlling, hard-handed father who made life difficult. I'm sure that his upbringing had a great deal to do with how he handled himself in relationships. When he found out I was pregnant, he asked me to marry him. I could not give him an answer for a month. I did not really want to marry this man but I struggled with making the decision. I thought, in the end, it would be the right thing to do so my children would have a father and I would have a husband who could help take care of everything.

The day we got married was the day he started to show his true colors. He had his license. He became very controlling of the girls and me. The girls were required to do all the household cleaning and, if not to his satisfaction, he would make them do it again. He became the disciplinarian and he was very strict. I did my best to protect the girls, sometimes pitching in and helping while he was away then lying to him so they would stay out of trouble. After our son was born, he did not allow me to breastfeed as this would interfere with his sexual pleasures. His daughter, from a previous marriage, came to live with us. She helped watch after the children while my husband would monopolize my time doing things he wanted to do; mostly fishing and hunting. Our drinking escalated. A co-worker came to live with us temporarily and we engaged in fulfilling my husband's sexual fantasies. The children would run and hide in their bedroom when he came home from working. I tried to be the mediator but somehow never managed to satisfy everyone. He became so controlling and so intimidating with threats of taking my children away, among other things. He was sexually and emotionally abusive. He had my girls and I parading around the house naked. At one point, he and his daughter had been arguing, he grabbed her and pushed her up against the wall. I tried to intervene and then he and I got into an argument. He ripped the phone out of the wall then took a painting down from the wall and broke the glass and started tearing the painting as he knew it was something I liked, treasured even. The argument escalated and he got a rifle. I told his daughter to run to the neighbor and call the sheriff. The sheriff arrived but couldn't remove my husband from the house unless he'd actually fired the rifle at me. The sheriff offered to escort me and the children out of the house if I chose to go. I chose to stay instead. Somehow, things calmed down and I avoided getting shot.

I had become afraid of him and what he might do. I was afraid for my children and at the same time, angry with myself for getting us into this situation. At one point, I went to a counselor telling her I was miserable in my marriage and wanted to know what I could do. She asked about our alcohol consumption. I was not entirely honest and felt like she just didn't get it. Alcohol wasn't the problem, my husband was. Of course, I now know better. Alcohol was a big part of the problem. We were both active alcoholics.

I had purchased a young horse and was making payments. This horse was everything to me. I felt as though she was my soulmate. I could spend time with her and everything was wonderful. At one point however, cash was tight and my husband told me I'd have to sell the horse or go out and prostitute myself to come up with the money to pay for her. I actually got dressed and drove away crying, knowing I couldn't do it, but I was trying to make him think I would. I returned of course, without having turned a trick.

We got a dog together; a rottweiler who he named Killer of Jews. We called her Killer. He knew I didn't like the name but of course, he insisted that this is what her name would be. He used a big tow-

110

chain as her collar and she stayed outside tied up. If she didn't obey, he would get angry with her. Once he kicked her so hard, I was sure he'd broken ribs. I hated the way he treated her. She didn't deserve it but once again, fear kept me from acting.

Another time, he was trying to get my son to say something and was making him squirm. He wanted him to say, 'The only good gook is a dead gook.' I was objecting and of course this was confusing to our son but he gave in and sheepishly said it to avoid his father's wrath. I was livid! I did not want our son to grow up this way.

When I'd finally had enough, I hired an attorney, with the help of my parents, got a restraining order and had him removed from the house. I stayed with my parents for several days. He moved to the house next door. He continued to try to intimidate me by standing at the end of the road and 'shooting his finger' at me as I drove by. The restraining order didn't do much. He knew just how far he could push it. I knew he wasn't stable and could easily have become violent. I can only thank God that he didn't.

I filed for divorce, which became final the following year. After trying very hard to discredit me and make my life as difficult as possible by reporting me to the department of motor vehicles and the IRS he finally moved out of town. I had to provide medical proof to the DMV that I was fit to drive and I ended up paying the IRS over $5,000 in taxes. He still had visitation rights with our son but those visits became more infrequent. I always feared he would try to flee with our son.

I got sober after our divorce and eventually moved out of state, looking for better opportunities for myself and my three children. My ex-husband died of a massive coronary about three years later.

It has taken me quite a bit of sober recovery time to come to realize that I played a role in my life and the men in my life were not wholly to blame for my misery. I was finally able to come to a place of forgiveness for all of us. It does not mean I forgive actions, but I can forgive their humanness. We are all somewhat sick. Some more than others. We all only do what we know how to do to the best of our abilities. I am grateful for my sobriety today and that I have learned so much about myself and the way I do relationships. My recovery has taught me how to do relationships differently. I do not have to rely on being okay if only someone else does things in a different way. I am the one who needs to change. I am the one who needs to stand up for myself. I am the one who needs to do it different. More importantly, I know I am able in all things with God's help.

My children have all grown up to be wonderful, loving, responsible adults. I have a relationship with my stepdaughter to this day. All of my girls have children of their own. I am happily married now for four years. I've retired from a nearly twenty-year career as a veterinary receptionist and I am loving my life!

SARAH

I was born in a small city but moved to a bigger one when I was four-years-old. I was raised in that big city by my mom and my dad. While living there, I went through things that a little girl should not have experienced!

My mom always worked twelve-hour shifts at night and so did my dad. So, we had a sitter, at this house, the people felt like family. But when I was nine-years-old, their uncle touched me in very inappropriate ways. I told my sitter and her sister what their uncle did but they didn't believe me. So, I didn't tell my parents, they had too much going on and I didn't want to add to those issues. My mom was a victim of domestic violence herself. Before I had any siblings and after my siblings were born, I saw my dad beat on my mom for things he did wrong. I saw her battered and heard her get emotionally and verbally abused. Arguments and fights went on for years until my mom stopped one night and just started praying for him to stop hitting her very loudly, she called on God and Jesus and my dad did not hit her again.

However, the verbal and emotional abuse continued, all together she stayed with him for twenty-five years before she got out. He had two other children (daughter's) with other women. Four children by three women and I am the oldest of all the kids. My sister came to live with us for five years, I don't know how my mom did that but I'm so glad she let my little sister live with us, even though that meant getting back with my dad. She is a very strong woman. My other sister stayed with her mom, but we all played together and we were raised as brothers and sisters, not half-sister, not half-brother! We are siblings just like everyone else. I love them all the same.

Thank God, my dad did make some big changes in his life and he has a very nice wife and he is a much better person. I love the changes that he has made and the fact that he is no longer violent and has not been for many years now. We get a long so much better now, especially over the last ten years.

By the time I reached ninth grade, I guess I started looking for love in all the wrong places. In high school, before I left the big city, I tried to have a boyfriend but just got cheated on. Summer before I started tenth grade, my family moved back to the small town I was born in, to be close to our family. This is where my nightmare of a love story began.

The guy I fell in love was not the guy I thought he was. I ran away from home with him, we were two hours away from my hometown when, one night, he left me alone in the apartment while he went to party with his friends. I was sleeping when I woke to find his uncle on top of me, I had flashbacks to when I was nine, but this time I was sixteen and was able to fight back and escape from the apartment before he was able to touch me again. I could only find a cold, dark corner to hide in, so I crawled in and cried for hours. The next day, my so-called boyfriend, who had made me run away from my family, told me to go back home. Back to my hometown where I had been on the news as a runaway, where I had been caught by the police as a runaway, I ran away again. I was scared that my mom would beat me, as she often did, or that she would kill me, as she had threatened when I did wrong things.

Now though, I was hard headed and did not listen. I used to sneak out of the house all the time and would run away when I was caught, because I knew that ever since my dad used to beat on my mom, she would then beat on me. Not a spanking. I was in high school when I went to the group home for being a runaway for the fourth time.

The relationship I mentioned had continued as this guy became the father of my children. When I was four-months pregnant with my first child, my daughter, I found out that another girl was also pregnant by my so-called boyfriend. There were arguments and almost fights between her and I, for many years to come.

My daughter was born and then her daughter was born four months later and they both looked just like him.

I left the group home before I gave birth to my daughter. Since the group home did not allow babies, I moved back home with my parents. I lived with them for about six months and the day I turned eighteen, I moved in with him and his mom. I did things I had no business doing to try and keep him and to avoid getting hit by him. The hitting started and I just thought it would stop. After my son was born, when I was twenty, I found out about his crack cocaine habit. And that was when the verbal, physical, and mental abuse started but I didn't know what it was. I felt like I did something wrong or that I caused the problem. I was very good to him. He would beat me up when he cheated, when he wanted money for his drug habit, he would beat me when he thought I was cheating. But it was really him cheating and his guilty conscience wanting to leave and go do drugs. I would come home from work or from being out with a friend and he would be in my house hiding and then start punching me in the arms, legs, slapping me in the face and his favourite, choking me. He would threaten to kill me, over and over again, if I left him. I was brainwashed and thought I had to stay for the sake of having a family with a mom and dad. There were times that my sister or my cousins would have to jump on him to get him off me because wherever we were, he would jump out of bushes and attack me.

I was scared of bushes for a long time.

I hid the bruises and the black eyes from my family. There were times I was not allowed around anyone, not even my sister, which I had to argue about every time. I was not allowed to go to some family functions, just work and take care of the children all by myself as he just did whatever he wanted.

He broke into my house too many times for me to count. One night he broke in and tied me up all night long. I thought I was dead. He was high on drugs and fell asleep. In the morning, he heard the kids get up and I lied to him saying that I had to ring my dad and tell him not to come and pick them up. Instead, I called the police, I left the door unlocked and went back to the bedroom where he tied me back up. The police arrived and found me tied up and off to jail he went.

So, finally, after nine years of being beat on by him, I had had enough!

I was no stranger to domestic violence, I lived it. With my mom, when we used to go to a friend's house to hide out, but she always went back.

115

The night I was being beat on and my daughter walked in to see me being choked on the ground, I yelled for her to go and call the police, told her that the neighbour is waiting … the fear in my baby girl's eyes and her screams of confusion as she was trying to figure out who to listen to – me screaming for help or her dad who is telling her not to open the door! I had already told my neighbour that I was going to send my daughter to use the phone as if I tried to use our phones he would rip the them all out of the walls, there were no cell phones back then.

The next thing I know, he is jumping out of bushes everywhere I went again.

The tenth year, I fought back and started calling the police every time he broke into my house and attacked me. I started getting really scared that he would kill me. So, I got a restraining order but he kept coming back.

Next, I went to CODA to get help getting a 'no contact' order against him. After the police finally caught him on my property, violating the order, he was put in jail for six months. So, while he was in prison, I started seeing a therapist who helped me find me and realise that I did not deserve to be beat on and that I was not only going through physical abuse but verbal and mental abuse too. I had no clue what she was on about. Mental abuse? Depression? I was just trying to get him off the drugs. The therapist kept stressing to me that his abuse was more than physical and that verbal and psychological abuse are just as harmful. She helped me believe that I could overcome the mental control and verbal abuse and see that I was strong enough to leave him for good.

Like many women in these situations, I stayed and I kept going back because I believed he had changed, I believed that he was sorry, until he would do drugs again or beat on me. He stole money from me and my kids for his habit. I was terrified of what would happen if I left.

I wish it hadn't taken me ten years to get out. I went through so many different things that I did not have to go through. Abuse that I should not have taken. Because I knew what that life was like for us all.

My mom told me that history was repeating itself, so I chose to break the cycle of abuse. I even had to wake up and realise that I was beating on my own kids and I had to stop and find other ways of punishment for them.

All of this caused me to develop generalised anxiety disorder, where I excessively worry about everything. I have anxiety and panic attacks but not as bad as I used to. I suffered from depression for so many years and had other problems processing things mentally. This has also changed me to be very protective of myself so I can become mean and angry. I have to yell and cuss at him now when he comes around now and tries to bother me. He knows he doesn't want to go back to prison because I will call the police.

My life still feels threatened by him because I can never forget all the beatings and the choking, threatening my life.

I am glad I finally left him with the help of CODA. Because I'm so happy with my new husband of ten years!

I have learned to love me, myself first and I know what I will not accept, no verbal, physical, or mental abuse from anyone. I'm so blessed to have my husband by my side to support me in everything I do. And he loves me for the person I am, along with the things I've been through. He doesn't make me worry about any hurt, harm, or danger coming to me from him. My husband is so nice and so sweet and has never hit me, not ever come close to hitting me. He doesn't like any types of violence, especially domestic violence. I've learned that finding love in the wrong place has hurt my kids and their future. I love me enough to be happy and have joy without a man in my life.

Love yourself first. Know your worth. Your life and your kids' lives depend on it.

Once you are stronger they will be strong enough not to go through the same cycle of abuse. I broke three cycles of abuse, you can do the same. Break one cycle and then break the next cycle. Life is so much better and peaceful. Reach out for help, find you and happiness will come to you.

Ask for help safely.

CHARLOTTE

I met my ex when my daughter was three months old, he was a couple of years younger than me. For fifteen months' we dated and I had no clue that he was what he was as he was kind, generous, loving, helpful, and loved being a 'dad'.

The problems started when we moved in together, he was away at university but also working when he was home. I was working full-time, paying the bills, paying the insurance on his car etc.

I remember the first violent attack, it was a weekend, the weather was warm, the house was clean. His golf bag was in the corner of the living room, my daughter was asleep. He was supposed to be going out but friends had cancelled, he quite quickly became verbally aggressive, I tried to appease him to keep my daughter sleeping, but nothing that I said or did would calm him, if anything, it infuriated him more. He was scaring me so I told him I was going around to my friend's house with my daughter, he picked up the golf bag and forced me against the wall with it, the bag was moved up (with the irons) to my neck, he was pressing on it. I was crying but luckily, my daughter stayed asleep. I told him to put the bag down, he snapped out of his fury and couldn't apologise more. He let me leave with my daughter but begged me to go back. Unfortunately, I did, I believed he wouldn't do anything like that again – instead what he did was much worse. I suffered broken fingers, hands, was punched everywhere that people couldn't see, was mentally abused on a daily basis, sexually abused whenever he could. He preyed on my emotions, pretended that he cared and that he loved me, only to hit me, shout at me and abuse me in any way he could. I phoned the police lots of times but never pressed charges … I believed that he loved me and he wouldn't do it again. Every time he did but he did something worse.

It took me nine years but I walked out on him, only to have him try to control things in my life after that.

I'm lucky, I have my life and I'm now married to a fantastic man who loves me for me, we have our arguments like everyone does but due to what I went through I often wonder if he'll do the same to me – all because of the person who put me through nine years of horrific mental, physical, and sexual abuse.

DEONNE MARSDEN

In June 1994 whilst at my mum's house, an argument started and Peter punched me in the head and face. My mum witnessed this and pulled Peter off me so he turned on my mum, hitting her too.

October 1995, our now eighteen-year-old son, was only a new born baby, Peter and I argued. I was working full-time within four weeks of having our baby, Peter had lost his job due to him stealing. On the day we argued, he punched the living room door and then ripped it off its hinges. I called his father and brother to come and calm him down but when they arrived, Peter threw his brother across the room too.

A couple of years later we were moving to a new house, from one side of town to the other, we had three children at this point, aged six-weeks, twenty-one months and three and a half. Peter lost his temper as I hadn't packed a box to his liking, he lashed out giving me a black eye and bruising on my cheek.

After an argument the following year, at my parent's house, Peter walked out so I followed him home. When I arrived, I saw him pull the locked patio door out of the frame and throw it ten-feet down the length of the garden in a fit of rage. I followed him into the house, followed by my mother and he started attacking me. My mum tried to stop him and he grabbed her by the neck, lifted her off the floor and proceeded to punch her too. My mum is only 5 feet 2 and has a tiny frame.

In 2001, on a caravan holiday in Withernsea, I was cooking Sunday dinner and the food was nearly ready. Peter asked me if I had made roast potatoes, when I explained that I hadn't and the food was nearly ready so it was too late to make them, he hit the roof, started screaming and shouting and hitting me, then he disappeared for over an hour. I went out looking for him with the children and we found him lying on a large, unstable rock in the sea near the cliff edge, asleep. When I tried shouting him, he wouldn't acknowledge me, finally he listened when I began to try climb to the rocks he was laid on. He told me he was going to fall asleep and was trying to drown himself. Obviously, I was upset, our children were watching from the cliff and I was crying at him not to be so stupid, he was being selfish and we could sort it out if he'd just come back and we call calmed down. After a while, he agreed to return to the caravan and I agreed to make him roast potatoes to calm him down.

In January 2010, we were living in Tingley when we argued over money and work. Peter ended up attacking me and ripping two doors from their hinges – in the lounge and dining room – the children were in bed. I left the house, got in the car and drove. My eldest two sons called Michael, Peter's brother, to come and calm him down, Michael tried calling me to convince me to return but I told him I was too scared and I was leaving for good. Then my eldest daughter called to see if I was okay and to tell me that the two youngest children were upset. I told her that I needed them to stay in their bedroom and keep safe and as soon as I knew it was safe, I'd be back to collect them all. My daughter suggested that she would try and lower herself and the younger two out of their bedroom window so that Peter wouldn't see them, if I would go back for them. Knowing that they were prepared to put themselves in danger to escape him really frightened me so I decided I had to return to look after them.

One evening in June 2010, Peter and I had gone for a drink together to our local pub. I tried explaining to him that he had had too much to drink and we needed to go home, I felt we had both had enough. Peter disagreed so I left alone, shortly after, he followed and an argument erupted. He told me to shut up or he would punch me, I said he needed to listen to me, he then punched me several times in the left eye, causing severe bruising and swelling. Once he had calmed down, I bathed the area and realised I couldn't see out of that eye. I took a couple of days off work and covered the bruising with make-up. His father saw what he had done and told him he shouldn't lose his temper – that was it.

A year later, June 2011, we were sat as a family, eating pizzas I had made. Peter was eating greedily and had eaten far more than anyone else so I told him to calm down and let the children have some more.

121

He got annoyed and pushed the pizza away, then lost his temper, asking me why I wasn't eating what was in front of me, I explained that the needs of the children were more important than mine and then he really lost his temper. He shouted at the children to go to bed, threw the table across the room towards the patio door, the pizza went everywhere, all over the wall and curtains; to get out of his way I started to clean it up but he followed me and punched me against the wall repeatedly. The children could hear me screaming and were very upset and frightened.

The following month, we had a family BBQ, we had all been drinking and I admit that I had had too much. I began to lean against Peter's cousin's ex-husband and innocently put my hand on his thigh, the next thing I knew, Peter had hold of me by my hair, dragged me across the lounge area and literally threw me outside in to a table and then jumped on me, punching me in the head, then, armed with a lump hammer, Peter went back in to the house and started shouting at and threatening the other man, he went to leave, but being drunk he couldn't drive but he was so scared he allowed his sixteen-year-old son to break the law just so they could get away. My children saw all this, they were only eight and ten at the time and were screaming, understandably traumatised.

That year, at our Christmas party, our sixteen-year-old son took a girl to his bedroom, we were under the impression they were being intimate and I didn't feel that this was appropriate so I asked Peter to go and tell him to come back downstairs. People were starting to ask where my son was. The next thing I knew, Peter had forced his way into our son's room, dragged him out and thrown him down the stairs, leaving the poor girl terrified.

In May 2012, our son was being a typical sixteen-year-old, mouthing back and being cheeky when Peter sent him to his room, my mum was staying at the time and had heard the argument and made her way to my son's room to calm him down. Peter had followed them and forced his way in, grabbed our son by his hair and started punching him in his head. My mum screamed and I ran up to them, we managed to drag Peter off him by threatening to call the police. My son and I left the house while he calmed down, when we got back, nothing more was said about it.

Later that year, August, I wasn't feeling very well so went to bed, I had recently undergone a cervical colposcopy examination due to abnormal cells, Peter wanted sex that evening but I said no. Peter's grandfather had recently died of cancer so that was making me even more worried. Peter started an argument and tried to drag me out of the bed naked, saying he was throwing me out on the street naked. I knew I needed to leave so the next morning I packed a bag and secretly hid it, in case anything happened again.

At the time, we owned a house in Leeds which was empty. I had been staying there whilst I decorated it and got it ready to rent out again. I decided I was safer leaving Peter so I began to sneak mine and the children's belongings out of the house. I told Peter I was leaving him and that I was moving back to Leeds and that I wanted a divorce. I got a solicitor and took the advice to file for divorce.

The funeral for Peter's grandfather was arranged, I had been with Peter since I was fifteen so his grandfather and I thought a lot about each other but Peter told me that I wasn't welcome to the funeral unless I put my wedding ring back on and moved back into the family home. I explained that we were over, that either I left or he did as I was not going to put up with him any longer. I finally had a house to live in and I was free and safe from the manipulation and abuse I had had put up with for years and years.

The next thing I knew I was receiving messages and calls from Peter threatening that if I didn't return home, I wouldn't ever see my children again and he would burn down the house I was staying in so that I had nowhere to go.

I was scared and frightened, he had control over me again and so, under sufferance, I went back home to work out another way to escape him and the violence.

I had been a registered childminder since 2004 and needed my house for my work. Each time I'd try to leave, Peter's family, although fully aware of the violence, always backed him up.

I was finally offered a job in January 2013, as a teaching assistant at a local school, I saw my chance to leave and support myself financially.

I told Peter I was leaving him as I couldn't take the arguments and the violence any longer, and I knew if I stayed much longer mine and my children's lives would be at risk.

In the January of 2013, I had a hospital appointment regarding my cervical smear which Peter took me to and picked up from. I was advised by the hospital to go home and rest, he took me to the family home and I slept for most of the afternoon. When I woke I went to call my employer to update them about whether I'd be in the next day when I found that my phone didn't work. I called T-Mobile only to be informed that my husband had changed all the passwords and terminated my contract, he had told them not to speak to me and not re-connect me!

I decided to go and drive to his work to find out what was going on only to discover my car was missing! I walked to his mum's house, up the road, to use her phone to call him and realised he had taken all the house keys too so I couldn't even leave the house. Very scared and worried, I walked to his mum's house and spoke to him, he told me he was on his way home so that we could talk, I went back to the house to wait for him.

When he arrived, he told me that, after speaking with his family, he had decided that if I was going to leave him, he was going to make it really difficult for me. He had disconnected my phone so that I had no contact with my parents or my friends to ask for help. I was totally dependent on him. He told me that whilst I had been in hospital earlier, he has sold my car, without my permission, and for a lot less than it was worth. We had a Range Rover which he had given me the previous year for my birthday but he had taken it to his dad's work for him to sell so that I couldn't have it.

Obviously, I was really upset.

But determined that this was it, I had to get away from this animal and his family, I went ahead and moved into my flat. A few days later we discussed bills etc. and agreed that he would pay off the debts with the money from the car sales. He froze the bank accounts without my knowledge, opened a new account and instructed the bank to transfer all funds credited to the old account directly into his new one, including taking all the family tax credits and child benefit payments, so that I financially suffered. He agreed to give me a car he had bought for £300.00 to sell on and make money on, as he knew I needed a car to collect the children.

His exact words at the time were, 'You leave me and I will make you suffer.'

I arranged to move into a flat and said I wanted the children to come and live with me too, he refused to let me see them, numerous arguments happened and I was more at risk if I stayed and argued so I decided to leave and consult my solicitor regards to custody of my children. I requested a divorce around this time too.

We had to share care of the children as he would not let them live with me, but he wasn't looking after them, the older children were taking the younger ones to and from school, they were also feeding them as Peter went straight to the pub after work and left the children alone till around 7.00 p.m. every night.

This is when I started letting social care know my concerns, every time I saw the children they had head lice, were unclean and complained of being hungry as they were living off microwave pizzas and other such foods that my fifteen-year-old daughter was capable of cooking.

Peter started dating his current partner in February 2013 and was staying out all night at her house after drinking too much in the pub with her. So, the two younger children were left overnight with my fifteen-year-old daughter looking after them. On a few occasions, she had called me asking if I knew where her dad was as he hadn't come home and she hadn't fed the children and she couldn't contact him.

My concerns for their welfare was growing as this was neglect.

In March 2013, I had the two younger children overnight and was returning them back to him after the visit, an argument started and he sent the children upstairs so that I couldn't take them back as I said I was keeping them in my care. As I went to leave the house and turned my back on Peter, he grabbed my hair and pushed me with such force towards the car, he smashed my head off the car and started punching me in the head and smashing me against the door frame. I managed to get in to the car but he tried dragging me out saying that if I didn't get out he would report me and say that I had stolen it from him. I managed to drive away from him and drove to his dad's and explained what had happened, he wasn't bothered and his exact words were, as he looked across to Peter's mum and said, 'I've hit her numerous times and she knows where her place is!'

I was disgusted and told them that I had left Peter as the abuse cannot carry on. I left his dad's house and phoned the police and reported the assault. Peter was arrested and his father took the children to his house and wouldn't let me see them. He called social services and started a whole load of lies and abuse saying that I was an incapable mother etc. I was told that if I went ahead and pressed charges against Peter, I would be buried alive soon. The police went to my father in law's house and got me my children but out of fear I dropped the charges.

On 26 June 2013, Peter returned from his holiday to C'an Picafort with the older three children and I was having the younger two that night, so once I collected him and the children from the airport I drove him to my house where he had left his car parked. After we had talked about how the kids had been on holiday, he tried to tell me he had missed me and wanted to start again, he was sorry for his past and I was his world. He was going to end his relationship with his girlfriend as it was me he loved etc. etc. I doubted him as I had already seen the messages on his Facebook to her suggesting sexual acts and telling her I was trying to win him back!

Her accusations of me being a mad woman and him agreeing with her, yet he was stood trying to tell me he loved me and he had bought me perfume, a dress, jewellery, all from his holiday, because he loved me. Our eldest daughter left the house to go to her boyfriends and the younger two were playing in the garden on the trampoline I had bought them whilst they were on holiday. I went upstairs for something and as I stood at the bottom of the bed he grabbed my shorts and tried pulling them down, I tried resisting but I couldn't, he pushed me on the bed and proceeded to have sex with me. I just froze and asked him to stop but he wouldn't. I waited for him to stop and then got up, went downstairs to check on the children and tried to ignore what had happened. He left shortly after and kept telling me that he still loved me and we could try again to make the marriage work as I was all he had wanted whilst on holiday.

HE USED ME. MANIPULATED ME. PLAYED MIND GAMES. ONLY NOW WHEN I LOOK AT IT ALL IT AMOUNTS OT DOMESTIC ABUSE!!!

In early July, the younger children had stayed with me and Peter was due to collect them on 7 July, to take them to Flamingo Land with some of the older kids, his girlfriend, and her two children. My boyfriend at the time had stayed over on the Saturday night and Peter was due to arrive around 8.00 a.m. on the Sunday morning. Peter had text to say he was on his way so I told my boyfriend to stay in bed and took the children downstairs, I didn't want Peter to know about him yet. When Peter arrived, he sent the kids to the car and forced his way into the house, demanding to know who was upstairs, I told him no one and asked him to leave, he attacked me, trying to pull my skirt up, when I wouldn't let him he ripped it, pulling it down, then the tore off my underwear and threw it across the room before pinning me up against the hallway under-stairs cupboard, holding me by my throat and giving me mental abuse, calling me names of a sexual nature and then forcing his fingers inside me. I was crying and begging him to stop but he kept saying that I was his wife and he wouldn't stop until I had come (orgasmed) for him. Over and over I told him he was hurting me and cutting me with his finger nails, I told him this was rape, that I would report him to the police, he said, 'phone them and I'll tell them you claimed tax credits you weren't entitled to and that you have been on my Facebook account.'

Our seven-year-old daughter came inside at one point, he told her to wait in the 'fucking' car and then slammed the door in her face.

He constantly moved his hand from my vagina to my face, wiping it across my cheek whilst calling me vulgar names and then forcing me into the downstairs bathroom where he continued to interrogate me about who I had been seeing, asking me if 'his cock is bigger than mine? Is he younger? Better in bed?' He knew he was hurting me and I was crying the whole time, I kept repeating over and over that this was rape and begging him to get off me, he kept justifying it saying I was his wife and he was entitled to do this.

He finally stopped and walked into the kitchen and helped himself to a can of pop from the fridge. I begged him to leave, knowing that I would call the police as soon as he left, but he refused saying that he needed the children's birth certificates. I asked why as he already had their passports and he didn't need them. He kept demanding them so, to get rid of him, I just gave him them and then made an excuse that I needed to go and get electric tokens from the shop and tried forcing him towards the door. He finally left, put his can in my bin and got in the car. I locked the front door and walked out of the street as if to go to the shop and as he drove past me in the car, he wound the window down and said, 'thank you, you dirty slag.'

I was physically shaking and as soon as he was out of sight I called my boyfriend to explain what had happened. He said he had come downstairs and heard some of the arguing but didn't know where the children where and didn't want to make even more of a scene in front of them. I was so shaken and disoriented that I just cried and asked him to get me away from the house. When I explained all of what had happened, he insisted that I call the police and have Peter arrested for rape but all I could care about was the children being in his care. If he was arrested that day, the children would see it all.

I was especially scared as social care had warned me not to make any more problems with Peter as it was affecting the children. I was scared.

I called my mum and good friend, both of whom told me to go to the police, but I had gone to my boyfriend's mum's caravan on the east coast by this point and I was safe. I called the police the following morning, once I knew I could collect the children from school and they would be safe. Once I explained to the police what had happened, and his violent past, Peter was arrested.

After a year on bail, the police have dropped the charges against him due to a lack of evidence.

I know what happened that day, I know I cried and cried at Peter to stop as he was hurting me and it was rape. Yet he continued.

I was offered no support or counselling. The Crown Prosecution Service told me not to take this matter any further as I would be dragged through the courts and interrogated about why I had never reported his physical assaults and torture. They told me I wouldn't be believed and the court ordeal would be traumatic – that I was best to move on and rebuild my life.

Knowing that he will never be punished for the abuse I suffered for twenty years will never leave my mind or allow me to move on. I've been physically free of him for four years, but mentally, he will hold me prisoner in my mind forever.

SPOTTING THE DIFFERENCE

As this book comes to an end I want to offer hope to those who have experienced abuse and feel that distinctive lack of trust for anyone, especially someone who you may consider having a relationship with. The honest truth is that there are others out there that are not out to hurt you or do you harm and you can have a healthy relationship with someone.

Knowing about a healthy relationship and what makes up the profile of that it:

- Respect – listening non-judgementally and valuing opinions
- Trust and support – supporting goals
- Honesty and accountability – accepting responsibility for self, admitting being wrong, communicating openly and truthfully
- Responsible parenting – sharing parental responsibilities, being a positive role model for the children
- Shared responsibility – mutually agreeing on a fair distribution of work, making family decisions together
- Economic partnership – negotiation and fairness and non-threatening behaviour
- Negotiation and fairness – Mutually satisfying resolutions to conflict, accepting change, willing to compromise
- Non-threatening behaviour – Talking and acting so that your partner feels safe and comfortable *

Aside from this educating yourself on the warning signs of abuse;

- If they cut you off from friends and family
- Threatening to hurt you or people close to you if you leave
- They monitor your movements

- Criticises you – constantly blames you for the abuse
- Forces you to have sex with them
- Controls your life: Money, who you see, what you wear
- They change mood suddenly from 'charmer' to 'monster'
- Humiliates you in front of others
- Says you're useless and couldn't cope without them
- Intimidates you into doing what they want
- Makes you change your behaviour to avoid making them angry**

It all may look like a lot to look out for but being knowledgeable will help and it has certainly helped me personally. I hope you find this next glimmer into my own life experience helpful as well.

* https://www.theduluthmodel.org/what-is-the-duluth-model/ (not direct quote but used to build the information together)

** http://metro.co.uk/2017/08/04/video-reveals-the-12-signs-that-youre-a-victim-of-domestic-abuse-6828340/

DOMESTIC ABUSE
LEARNING TO LOVE AND TRUST AGAIN

Taking those first steps back into the 'real' world after moving on from an abusive relationship can be very disconcerting. Those first few months bring to the fore the realisation of what you have just been put through and finding the confidence to make informed choices for yourself requires resilience and courage. It is certainly not easy and I personally spent a lot of the time questioning myself and my decisions. Who can you trust? Who can you talk to? Can I see my friends again? Will someone be watching me? Am I doing the right thing? Do I need someone else's approval?

I was very lucky to have found a friend in my (now) husband. He really didn't have it easy when we started our relationship. In fact, there can be still moments now that I struggle to feel relaxed and confident. Ultimately, he helped to pick up the broken pieces and spent a long time helping me to put them back together again. Make no mistake, it wasn't simple and there's no instruction manual or picture to refer to, he spent a lot of time guessing and trying to not make a wrong step as I worked my way through some fairly complex issues. I know if you asked him, he would tell you in a heartbeat that it was worth it but even I can see just how much he had to go through to earn my trust and to be able to put aside my negative thoughts of the past. Having a 'friend' has helped me enormously on the journey to being the person I always knew (deep down) I was but who had been hidden from sight by the effects of an abusive and coercive relationship.

In trying to offer some help, I suggest that if you're trying to support a survivor that these steps may help:

1. Listen

2. Try to understand – don't make the other person feel unusual.

3. Keep calm – it's going to take time and most likely months if not years.

4. Actions speak louder than words – if you make those promises, then stick to them.

5. Be affectionate – Often this is not paramount in the abusive relationship and affection is important as it releases the positive hormones, builds trust, and reduces stress.

6. Take things at his/her own pace and not force him/her to move on with the relationship faster, sexually, or emotionally.

7. Playing devil's advocate – in an appropriate away as this allows him/her to realise how they are coming across, examples include asking permission to go to the toilet, when/if they may eat, or speak to friends.

8. In my opinion, without trust there is no love (in its broadest sense) and without that there is no foundation for a healthy relationship.

One of my favourite quotes of all times is: 'The greatest thing you will ever learn, is just to love and be loved in return'. When I was in the abusive relationship I never appreciated what this really meant and I felt that I was giving everything of me to my abuser but I was ultimately gaining nothing back.

Thankfully as time moves on, more ways of addressing abuse are being developed such as The Domestic Violence Disclosure Scheme. This gives members of the public a 'right to ask' the police when they have a concern that their partner may pose a risk to them or where they are concerned that the partner of a member of their family or a friend may pose a risk to that individual. If an application is made under the scheme, police and partner agencies will carry out checks and if they show that the partner has a record of abusive offences, or there is other information to indicate that there may be a risk from the partner, the police will consider sharing this information.

Moving forward is hard and sometimes the abuse will come back in dreams, flashbacks, conversations or in other ways. I find that sometimes it feels like I am in a mental fight not to assume my husband is similar to the person who abused me. Years on and the moments have become less and I am able to shake it off, but this has taken patience and has at times been mentally quite tough.

So, my message to you today is that you can learn to love and trust again. The road may be difficult and sometimes challenging but it's worth it!

Jennifer Gilmour

ACKNOWLEDGEMENTS

Thank you first to Emma Mitchell, who has spent the time to edit *Clipped Wings* and in keeping the survivor's voice, lots of emails back and forth so that those who have given their story are happy with those small changes. Emma has not only edited but she has given her welcomed thoughts as I felt it was important to get this right.

Thank you to Georgina Preston from Savannah Rose Digital who has worked with me on my imagination for the book cover, she brought my thoughts, notes, and sketches to life and truly knew the direction of *Clipped Wings*.

Thank you to book bloggers – without your support I would at times feel like I am talking to myself in the land of media. Never think your role isn't important because you motivate, encourage and inspire writers to continue in their work. A special thanks to Jessica Page Johnson from Jessica's Reading Room, Abbie Rutherford from Bloomin' Brilliant Books, Meggy Roussel from Chocolate 'n' Waffles, Anne Cater from Random Things Through My Letter Box, Wendy Clarke from Fiction Café; you have been with me right from the beginning of my release of *Isolation Junction* and your honest feedback and your support will never be forgotten. Thank you also to John Redhead for helping to get this book ready for print.

Thank you to fellow authors who continue to inspire me and motivate me to continue in my journey.

Thank you to readers and followers on social media, without your virtual support in engaging with my posts the message wouldn't be read and you help spread the awareness of domestic abuse and that it isn't acceptable.

Thank you to those who supported by pledging in the Kickstarter campaign which took place in August and September 2017. Without your support, those who have given their story would be without a copy of Clipped Wings.

THANK YOU TO THE FOLLOWING PEOPLE
WHO PLEDGED THEIR SUPPORT:

Amanda McCormick

Beat Muellor

Bernadette Barlow

Burt Jarratt

Caroline Aitken

Diane Parnham. A New Horizon-Coaching Services

Di Davenport & Barry Palmer

Dorota Niecikowska

Elyse Buell

Erin Gienger

Irene Furbur

Jackie Woolnough

Jaelithe Leigh-Brown, Mrs Mojo

Jenna Jones

Jessica Page Johnson

Jo Howarth

John Redhead

Jude Lennon

Julie Aldcroft

Justyna Cieslinska

Hannah Copeland

Hannah Maiden

Michala Leyland, Wood for The Trees Coaching

Michele Stevenson

Michelle Emma Ogborne

Nicci Simmonds

Robin Gilmour

Roger Davies

Sarah Brock

Sharon Kearns

Sharon Bosker

Stephanie Hemsted

Sue Blaylock

Tina (Purple Nanny) Raymond

Tracey F

Vicki Sparks

And to those who pledged but wanted to remain anonymous, massive thanks to you too.

Without the support of my husband, I wouldn't be where I am today and even though he would not want this recognition, I feel it is important to mention him. The support he gave me after an abusive relationship, at what was undoubtedly the most vital time that I needed someone by my side. A friend at the time I most needed one, who held my hair whilst I was being sick, who cared for me, and held me up when I couldn't. To his love and care years later when he still listens to me and takes my worries away.

A love I thought I would never find.

For this, my love, I write to you;

LEARNING TO LOVE AGAIN

I never thought that I would find,
Someone who loves me back and is always kind,
For I was lost and you found me,
You broke me free from what bound me,
You helped me learn to love again,
To trust and open up and have no shame,
You're my hero and knight,
And now I want you to know that you don't need to fight,
You don't need to hold me up when I feel so much pain,
Because now we hold each other's hands and through this turmoil
we have gained,
A love that is so strong, unbreakable and pure,
One that can stand tall and be united to endure,
Thank you from the bottom of my heart,
And thank you for showing me that I could have a new start.

A NOTE TO THOSE WHO HAVE GIVEN THEIR STORY IN HERE

I personally want to commend you for your involvement with this project. Your story will help many and will save lives. It will educate others to see what abuse can look like, a job sometimes text books cannot do. You have given your voice a sound and it will be heard.

Your courage to speak out shows that you have come so far and I know you are still walking your journey but I hope it has brought some peace to your minds that you don't have to be trapped or be silenced.

Thank you for standing with me and others, together we are louder and stronger.

ABOUT THE AUTHOR

Born in the north-east, Jennifer is a young, married mum with three children. In addition to being an author, she is an entrepreneur, running a family business from her home-base. Her blog posts have a large readership of other young mums in business.

From an early age, Jennifer has had a passion for writing and started gathering ideas and plot lines from her teenage years. A passionate advocate for women in abusive relationships, she has drawn on her personal experiences to write her first novel *Isolation Junction*. It details the journey of a young woman from the despair of an emotionally abusive and unhappy marriage to develop the confidence to challenge and change her life and to love again.

Since the publication of her debut novel, Jennifer has continued to be an advocate for those in abusive relationships through her blog posts, radio interviews and Twitter feed. Jennifer also gained a qualification in facilitating a recover programme for those who have been in abusive relationships.

Jennifer continues to publicly support those who are isolated and struggle to have a voice. Jennifer hopes that *Clipped Wings* give's a voice to survivor's experiences and raise's awareness further of the types of unacceptable behaviour which fall into the category of domestic abuse.

A MESSAGE FROM THE AUTHOR

I hope that in reading these accounts, together we raise awareness of this often hidden and unseen behaviour and empower those in abusive relationships to seek help for themselves and find the confidence to change their lives.

If you have been affected by what you have read in this book, you are not alone, talk to someone and take the first step out of isolation. Or you can call the 24-hour free-phone National Domestic Violence helpline on 0808 2000 247.

There are national, local, charity, and council-led helplines, so I urge you to make that call, if it's safe.

If you are not in the UK, I am sure there are support lines of a similar nature.

Jennifer

www.JenniferGilmour.com
www.facebook.com/IsolationJunctionbook
www.twitter.com/JenLGilmour

REFERENCES

Life After Domestic Abuse

http://www.huffingtonpost.co.uk/jennifer-gilmour/life-after-domestic-abuse_b_9515764.html

and Learning to Love and Trust Again

http://www.huffingtonpost.co.uk/jennifer-gilmour/domestic-abuse_b_17090974.html

are articles originally posted on Huffington Post website by Jennifer Gilmour

ALSO BY JENNIFER GILMOUR

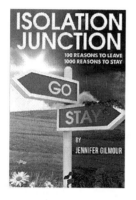

Rose is the mother of two young children, and finds herself living a robotic life with an abusive and controlling husband. While she struggles to maintain a calm front for the sake of her children, inside Rose is dying and trapped in 'Isolation Junction'.

She runs an online business from home, because Darren won't let her work outside the house. Through this, she meets other mums and finds courage to attend networking events, while Darren is at work, to promote her business.

It's at one of these events that Rose meets Tim, a sympathetic, dark-haired stranger who unwittingly becomes an important part of her survival.

After years of emotional abuse, of doubting her future and losing all self-confidence, Rose takes a stand. Finding herself distraught, alone and helpless, Rose wonders how she'll ever escape with her sanity and her children. With 100 reasons to leave and 1,000 reasons she can't, will she be able to do it?

Will Tim help her? Will Rose find peace and the happiness she deserves? Can Rose break free from this spiralling life she so desperately wants to change?

Made in the USA
Columbia, SC
27 May 2018